THE COMPLETE GUIDE TO SAINT BERNARDS

Jessica Dillon

LP Media Inc. Publishing

Text copyright © 2019 by LP Media Inc.

www.lpmedia.org

Publication Data

Jessica Dillon

The Complete Guide to Saint Bernards --- First edition.

Summary: "Successfully raising a Saint Bernard Dog from puppy to old age" --- Provided by publisher.

ISBN: 978-1-952069-01-7

[1. Saint Bernard Dogs --- Non-Fiction] I. Title.

Design by Sorin Rădulescu

First paperback edition, 2020

TABLE OF CONTENTS

CHAPTER 4
Bringing Home Your Saint Bernard

CHAPTER 5
Socializing Your Saint Bernard Puppy

CHAPTER 6
Living with a Large-Breed Puppy

*In memory of Vivian S. Sims and Callie H. Stevens,
the two woman who inspired me to write and love animals.*

INTRODUCTION
Bringing Home Tulip

Photo Courtesy of
Jessica Dillon

It was a hot summer day when we drove to a mall with a pet store in it. Puppies surrounded us, but none of them felt right and we couldn't bring ourselves to bring one home. My boyfriend, Johnathan, and I both had pets, but we had never really talked about adopting a dog together. After seeing the puppies, we both started to talk about what our dream dogs were. Saint Bernards came up pretty fast. I wanted a family friendly breed, Johnathan wanted a big dog to laze around the house.

We did some research online, found that a breeder a few hours away had just had a litter and emailed her to learn more. A few weeks later we were celebrating my birthday at a local arcade when the breeder texted me six pictures, each of a different puppy. I scrolled down and saw the puppy with the number three posted beside it. She was a little girl who had a perfect mask and was as fuzzy as could be. Long story short, we picked up our new puppy, Tulip, two weeks later.

Now, neither of us had ever raised a puppy on our own before, and Tulip was big. We took her to a pet store and purchased anything that piqued her interest. Two weeks later, she had already outgrown everything. Tulip also managed to pee on every bed we gave her. Puppy pads were a toy to her, and this quickly growing puppy wasn't old enough for bladder control. Tulip, to put it bluntly, was chaos incarnate.

Before long, we learned to schedule better, finding Tulip needed to be walked a lot. Our little ball of chaos started to blossom into a beautiful member of our family. In all honesty, Tulip helped us learn to work together as a couple. If one of us didn't communicate about Tulip's needs, then we knew we were going to have a mess to clean up. Furthermore, socializing Tulip got us out to places we'd rarely gone before, like the park.

Today, she always has to sit directly between us on the couch. If she can't touch both of us, then she instantly tries to readjust. When I'm working, Tulip is more than happy to just lay at my feet. From time to time, she even gets into watching movies with us though we've had to teach her not to bark at dogs on screen. We always know that when we go outside, she'll be right beside us. She doesn't even allow us to leave her sight!

Let me assure you, there is nothing better for an anxious individual than having a giant fuzzy dog guarding you. Not only do they ward off any trouble just by the sound of their mighty bark, but they will also nuzzle up against you the whole time. Tulip always lets us know when we have a visitor, even if it's just a small bunny rabbit grazing on some grass.

Even with all the puppy mess, chewed up toys, and constant collar purchases, we would go pick her up all over again. She is our family and one of the most loyal animals you could ever own. No matter how bad a day might be, I know that Tulip's fuzzy tail will be wagging every time I come home.

Photo Courtesy of
Jessica Dillon

CHAPTER 1
History of the Saint Bernard Breed

"Saint Bernards are a giant dog that has no clue just how large they really are."

Marilyn Balikowski
Cornerstone Saint Bernard Kennel

Saint Bernards have long captured the imagination of pet lovers for being incredibly loyal and caring dogs. The breed has a long history starting with the famous imagery of wearing barrels around their necks and the dogs' association with monks. Just where did these giant dogs come from, and why did someone feel the need to breed them?

The history behind the Saint Bernard is a heartwarming tale of human compassion. Everything about this breed was developed with human kindness in mind.

Photo Courtesy of
Denise Rosa

Photo Courtesy of Mary Baker

What Class of Dog Is a Saint Bernard?

Believe it or not, the often lazy Saint Bernard is a working dog. While you might not see a Saint pulling a sled or working as a police dog, they have a lot of potential. Working dogs, in general, are intelligent and quick to train. If properly trained, a Saint Bernard can be an excellent guard dog, though it needs plenty of discipline and repetition. The breed's sheer size, combined with Saints' willingness to protect their family, can cause trouble when not adequately trained. For example, there is nothing worse than having a hundred pound dog completely convinced that your mailman is trying to break into your house. Working dogs take an active approach to issues.

A Monk's Best Friend

Saint Bernards were first bred by monks at the Great St. Bernard Hospice, located in the Great St. Bernard Pass. The earliest records of the breed date back to 1707. The hospice also has artwork of Saint Bernards that date back to 1690. These canine helpers were able to withstand extreme cold and were willing to help find travelers who had gone missing in the mountains, becoming trapped during the snowfall common to the Alps where the monks lived.

The monks first imported Alpine Mastiffs, which eventually were bred into the Saints we know today. Bernards were so adept at their jobs that the younger dogs would learn how to rescue from the seniors. In fact, the monks never specifically trained the dogs in rescue. They learned on their own. This cycle took place for nearly 200 years before the dogs became a more domestic breed.

Sadly, in the 1800s the Alps suffered from several harsh winters and many Bernards were killed during rescues gone awry due to avalanches. To save the breed, the monks decided to cross the remaining Bernards with Newfoundlands. This resulted in the cross-bred Bernards having a heavier coat. Unfortunately, the heavy coats held in too much of the Alps moisture, slowing them down and leading to health complications. These heavy coats made them unfit for winter rescues, thereby ending that part of the Bernards' history.

Next, the dogs began to work with Swiss farmers to help protect their farms. This eventually led to the breed becoming more family-oriented. By 1884 the breed had grown in popularity and became the first breed to be recognized by the Swiss Studbook. These heroic dogs were also given the honor of being Sweden's national dog and still proudly represent the country today.

QUOTE

"The Saint Bernards work best in teams of at least three dogs. They are sent out on patrols following storms, and they wander the paths looking for stranded travelers. If they come upon a victim, two dogs lie down beside the person to keep him warm; one of the two licks his face to stimulate him back to consciousness. Meanwhile, another dog will have already started back to the hospice to sound the alarm."

Stanley Coren,
psychology professor and writer

Photo Courtesy of
Floyd Gingrich

Where Did the Barrel Myth Come From?

If you own a Saint Bernard, one of the things you will be asked around Halloween is, "are you putting a barrel on his neck?" Books, cartoons, and movies have cemented the image in people's minds of a heroic Saint Bernard carrying warming alcohol to stranded, freezing travelers. However, the truth is that the Bernards used for rescue were smaller than the ones today. They could never have carried giant, heavy barrels.

What exactly started this barrel myth though, and why is it so widely accepted as a fact? Well, as it turns out, a young teenager was the start of the legend. A 17-year-old boy named Edwin Landseer created a famous painting in 1820, Alpine Mastiffs Reanimating a Distressed Traveler, depicting two Saint Bernards. In the art piece, the dogs are standing over a fallen traveler. One Bernard is depicted wearing a barrel around their neck while the other is licking the injured man. The young man, when asked about the barrel, said that it contained brandy.

Photo Courtesy of
Kristen Carp

Famous Saint Bernards

Throughout the Saint Bernard's history in media, the breed has found its way into several famous productions. The most famous modern-day Saint is Beethoven, a lovable fictional dog that a series of kids movies were based around. Saint Bernard sales spiked each time a new movie in the franchise came out. Conversely, Cujo, a horror movie, depicted a crazed Saint Bernard and probably caused some people to become wary of the breed. Nana from Peter Pan is an excellent example of the breed's natural love for children.

QUOTE

"I'm Volstagg and what you see is what you get. He's a bon vivant, lover of life, epicurean good fellow. He's a god, which helps. He's full of life. He reminds me very much of Falstaff. There's a wonderful innocence to him and the steadfast loyalty of a big Saint Bernard dog. He'd come running through the snow with a keg of beer to save your life."

Ray Stevenson,
*Northern Irish actor who portrayed Volstagg in the 2011 film **Thor***

Saint Bernards have even made their way into video games like Sony's Detroit Become Human, where a police officer is depicted as owning a large Saint named Sumo. The Sims 3: Pets gives players the option to make their very own Saint. Even Japanese animation has found a place for the breed in the series Heidi, Girl of the Alps.

A Saint Bernard named Barry is said to have saved more than 40 people in the Alps before retiring to a life of leisure. Many stories are based around Barry's rescue efforts in the wintery mountains. These tales include a myth stating that the forty-first rescue killed Barry. Thankfully though, the truth is that Barry died of old age and was then preserved for future generations. Both his skull and pelt can be seen in The Museum of Natural History in Bern Switzerland.

These dogs have even made their way into sports becoming the mascot of the Cincinnati Reds and the New Orleans Saints. Saint Bernards are used in commercials by various companies. These commercials often use the dog's lazy nature to depict a sense of peace and calm.

*Photo Courtesy of
Renate Magnussen*

How Big Is the Average Puppy?

When we picked Tulip up at two months of age, she was roughly the size of a Shih-Tzu and weighed around 15 to 20 pounds already. It's pretty hard to understand just how young these puppies are just by looking at their size. Most Bernard puppies easily hit the 20-pound mark by the time they are three months of age. Some even weigh 30 plus pounds, and that isn't an uncommon occurrence. I remember when we first met our breeder and she plopped our puppy down in our arms, I was completely caught off guard at the weight.

Physical Appearance of a Saint Bernard

The Saint Bernard can be quickly identified from other giant breeds thanks to their prominent characteristics. You will immediately notice the droopy face and sad expression. Even the Saint Bernard's floppy ears are positioned high on their heads helping set the breed apart from other dogs. You will also notice the Saint Bernard appears naturally bulky and has a broad chest. Their tails are naturally curved and long, often reaching halfway to the ground.

The Saint Bernard can have a short or long coat. Either way, you will find that the coat is double layered to help keep the dog warm in the cold. Saint Bernards are usually covered in brown and white fur and commonly have a mask around their eyes. Common color combinations for a Saint Bernard's coat are red and white or brindle and white.

What Type of Temperament Does a Saint Bernard Have?

"Saints are loyal, laid back in nature, can be protective, like to snuggle, easy going, and oh yeah, they LOVE to eat."

Van and Beth Pankratz
Pankratz Puppies

Photo Courtesy of Henry Wojnarowski

Temperament should play a huge role in picking any dog breed. The truth is every breed is different; some dogs are going to lie at your feet while others spend most of their time playing. Saint Bernards aren't for people who want to be left alone. In fact, leaving them alone can cause them to become depressed. These dogs love to be by their family's side at all times. This temperament makes them a poor choice for an outside dog.

Photo Courtesy of Catherine Koutsoumbaris

Bernards are mostly humble giants that thrive off social interaction. They love being in a family and have earned their title "nanny dog" from their gentle nature around children. Many Saint Bernards find it easy to say hi to strangers, making them a questionable choice for guard dogs. Saint Bernards can often be goofy and find the simpler things in life pleasing. I had never actually seen a breed so stereotypically happy with a simple stick until I brought home Tulip.

If you want a sweet dog that will follow your every step, then this breed may be for you. Just keep in mind that Saint Bernards are incredibly people dependent and don't do well alone for long periods of time. Before you bring home your puppy, you should heavily consider how much time he will spend alone each day. Bernards are extremely sensitive and will need proper socialization to become good guard dogs.

How Big Should Your Home Be?

Johnathan and I live in a three-bedroom two-bath house with an average-sized kitchen and a large living room. Outside we have a yard surrounded by a woodline that's probably a little more than your standard high school football field. Before getting Tulip, we already had my two cats and an old hound dog named Nate, who mostly stayed on his couch.

When we brought Tulip home, we were worried she'd grow too large for us or that we'd have to keep her outside. We wondered if a hundred-plus pound Saint Bernard was going to be a titan who took over the house.

Photo Courtesy of
Deb Gioffredi

It turns out she's happy just sprawled on the floor, mainly in the living room, sleeping.

Even as a playful pup, Tulip never really needed that much space other than when she was outside. She doesn't even use the full yard; she is more than happy just to run laps around the house and carry sticks she finds. The only real issue we've had is when she follows us into a smaller room where her tail always tends to knock things over. While I don't recommend a tiny apartment setting, a standard two-bedroom residence is more than enough for a Bernard as long as it has a decent amount of space to run around outside. These dogs don't like to wander off and explore or exercise for extremely long periods of time. As long as they have room to sprawl out, Saint Bernards are more than happy just to be close to you.

Can You Afford to Get a Saint Bernard?

A Saint Bernard can cost over $500 a year, so it's important to consider your budget before getting a dog, whether a puppy or an adult. To begin with, let's look at adopting versus buying a Bernard. Buying a Saint Bernard tends to be around $1,000, and many shelters will have an adoption fee of around $250. Either way, this almost guarantees that your first-year costs will easily exceed the $1000 mark. Here is a breakdown of food, toys, supplies, and vet bills for the first year.

Expense	Cost
Food	$1,000
Toys	$100
Leash & Collar	$150
Crates	$200
Grooming	$170
Vet Bills	$250
Misc	$100
Total	**$1970**

We spent roughly $2,000 the first year just on getting the basics. Add in the $1000 we paid for her and we hit over $3,000 on the first year. Of course, variables like vet packages and individual dog needs can make this more or less expensive for you.

CHAPTER 2
Buying vs. Adopting a Saint Bernard

"Saint Bernards are generally extremely mellow. Known as 'the nanny' of dogs, they should be great in a family setting. They are very gentle and love their people."

Jillian Muir
Beech Hill Saints

O nce you've decided you're going to take the leap and get a Saint Bernard, you'll probably have a lot of questions about how to prepare for a puppy. As you do so, it's important to realize this isn't just a puppy, it's a very large puppy that will grow quickly. Based on the average price tag of a Saint Bernard, as discussed in the previous chapter, you may be wondering how to make sure you're not just throwing your hard-earned money into the wind. How do you make sure you take the right steps as you make this life-changing decision? We'll help you out.

Photo Courtesy of Kelsie Stull

Photo Courtesy of
Madison Curry

Rescue or Purchase?

The first thing you need to decide is if you want to buy a Saint Bernard from a breeder or adopt one from a shelter or rescue organization. Buying a Saint in many ways can be much simpler than adopting. You just find a breeder, verify that they are reputable, and then pick-up your puppy. Buying, of course, is always going to be more expensive and you're guaranteed to get a puppy unless you opt to buy a retired breeder. Either way, you are getting a dog of your choice with papers.

Adopting is a much more complicated process; it's not every day someone gets rid of their Saint Bernard. Some hopeful owners spend years waiting for a Saint Bernard to appear for adoption. Even then, they have to be approved and may end up driving for hours to pick up their new companion. These Saints aren't going to come with papers, even if the vet knows they're a pure breed. You also have a higher chance of getting an older dog instead of a puppy. Adopting is usually a cheaper option as most facilities will charge a quarter of the breed's cost.

Photo Courtesy of Cara Kells

Searching For a Breeder

To begin the process, find your breeder asking your vet for a reference, using the official AKC site, or by researching the websites of established breeders. Never use online classified ads or websites that let literally anybody list. Once you contact a breeder, cross-reference everything they say. Use the internet to research this person, use an image search to see if the pictures of the puppies came from somewhere else, and ask tons of questions. One of my favorite resources is using a phone book to match the name, phone number, and area of my potential breeder.

Finding the right breeder is probably the most anxiety-inducing part of buying a puppy. You have to trust a stranger unless you're fortunate enough to know a breeder. If you've never purchased a pet from a breeder before then here are some things you need to keep in mind before messaging a potential breeder:

- Most Breeders Require a Puppy Deposit
- Deposits Can Range Between $200 to $500 For Bernards
- The Puppies May Not Even Be Born Yet
- This Deposit is Usually Sent Online, Not Done in Person.
- Puppy Fraud Exists
- You Will Be Bound to a Contract
- The Puppy Has a Pick-Up Date
- Some Deposits Are Non-Refundable

Ask to read over the contract before you send money and never send more than half the cost of the dog. I also ask to speak with other buyers when possible, or I message them on Facebook if the kennel has a page. From my experience, most people who have bought from the breeder are more than happy to tell you if the purchase went well or not.

If the puppies aren't born yet, and the person doesn't have any references, then you should pass on buying a dog from them. You should also be cautious of any breeders who don't want to talk to you. Reputable breeders want to know who they are selling their puppies to and whether your home will be a good fit.

If possible, you should meet up with your puppy or at least see some young Saint Bernards before bringing one home. Meeting your puppy gives you a much better picture of what you're getting and keeps you from being stuck with dog supplies that are way too small.

Requirements of a Reputable Breeder

"You need to be careful to pick from a breeder that cares well for their animals. There are many breeders out there, both licensed and hobby breeders. It is a good idea to visit the breeder and see where and how the puppies are being raised. A pup that is being handled by people daily will adapt to their new home better than a puppy that isn't socialized with people."

Van and Beth Pankratz
Pankratz Puppies

Reputable dog breeders all share one goal: to progress and preserve their selected breed. Reputable breeders who abide by this common rule will never breed sick or distressed pets, and their sires and dams will have regular check-ups. Before breeding begins, the selected pair will be checked for genetic defects and current health problems. Only after a clean bill of health will a reputable breeder start the mating process.

Many reputable breeders will be able to provide paperwork, as they have registered with the AKC for both dogs. They should also register the puppies or give you the information to do so yourself. Reputable breeders understand the time, commitment, and possible complications of pregnancy. Because of this, contracts will forbid you from legally breeding your Saint Bernard unless you pay an additional fee.

Photo Courtesy of Marijh Khan

Health Tests and Certifications

All puppies should be taken to the vet by the breeder after they have been born. The vet will check them for health issues or possible genetic defects. After the puppies have a clean bill of health, that vet can certify that the puppies are in good health and ready to be adopted out to proper homes. Breeders should have a checklist to make sure the puppies will be in good health.

Saint Bernards should be checked for both hip and elbow defects. This is especially important as hip and joint problems are especially prevalent in large breeds as they age. The breeds' eyesight also needs to be checked for possible vision issues. A cardiac exam should also be performed to ensure the puppy's heart is beating regularly. The parents need to have proof of a degenerative myelopathy DNA test to guarantee spinal issues won't emerge in the puppies.

FUN FACT

Saint Bernard Rescue Foundation, Inc.

The Saint Bernard Rescue Foundation is an organization that assists Saint Bernards in need. From homeless dogs and those in abusive homes, to dogs who are injured, this foundation does not refuse services to any dog who may be in need, though their focus is on Saint Bernards. To fill out an adoption application, make a donation, read success stories, or purchase merchandise which supports the foundation, you can visit their website at saintrescue.org.

Breeder Contracts and Guarantees

Every reputable breeder has a contract outlining the requirements for purchasing a Saint Bernard. Though contracts vary from breeder to breeder, to start with, most contracts will state whether your deposit is refundable or not. Many breeders will make only a portion of your hold deposit for the puppy refundable. Next, the contract will probably state whether you can add on breeding or not. By purchasing breeding rights for an additional fee, you can legally breed your dog. Many breeders may choose not to sell breeding rights, and if you're caught breeding your dog they can take legal action against you that can cost you both money and ownership of your pet.

In fact, most contracts have clauses about the continued ownership of your Bernard. Your ownership can become forfeit if you leave your Saint out on a chain, don't keep up with vaccinations, or even don't properly groom your puppy. Many breeders will also have a clause saying the puppy is to be returned to them if for any reason you can't keep the animal.

Likewise, these contracts also include health guarantees. A health guarantee can assure that if your puppy becomes sick within 30 days or dies due to genetic issues within a year, you will get a refund or replacement. These guarantees can also ensure that you get your money back if you later learn that your puppy was never taken to the vet by the breeder.

How to Evaluate a Shelter or Rescue

If you've chosen to go the adoption route, then you can look to both shelters and rescues to find your Saint Bernard. You will need to make sure the place you're adopting from is a legitimate facility. Most of the time, finding a Saint Bernard for adoption means you will have to look hours away from your home. Sadly, some scammers take advantage of a person's efforts to give a dog a home. Likewise, some places claim to rescue purebred dogs, but are more concentrated on the profit that can come from adoption fees than actually finding a loving home for the dog.

To verify that the facility you're adopting your Saint Bernard from is legitimate there are a few steps you can take. First, check to make sure they have a sound adoption process and form. All legitimate adoptions should have a thorough process to weed out unqualified pet parents. Next, ask to tour the facility or find their business hours and stop by. Many adoption facilities will have hours for the public to come and meet the dogs. Having open facilities means more potential owners will connect with a pet and adopt it. Finally, check to see what shots/procedures your prospective dog has had. Most reputable adoption facilities will vaccinate and spay/neuter the pet.

Photo Courtesy of Kallie Brock

You should also check to see if a facility has ties to any national adoption organizations like the ASPCA. Another good idea is to check the county page where the rescue or shelter is located to see if they're mentioned. Most adoption organizations should be active in their community and you should be able to use social media to find a trail of events or other adoptees.

Choosing the Perfect Pup

Choosing the perfect Saint Bernard should be a relaxed experience. If you meet a Bernard, but don't feel sure about the dog, then it may not be the right pup for you. Every Saint Bernard has its own individual personality and temperament. Even in adoption situations, don't jump at the first available Bernard. You will want to take time, especially with an older dog, to decide if your home will meet the animal's needs. Be aware that if you adopt a Bernard with separation anxiety, a common affliction in rescues, then you can't be away from home frequently or for long periods of time.

Photo Courtesy of Bobbie Conrad

Be sure to go over all the quirks a puppy or grown Saint may have with the breeder or shelter. Reputable breeders and shelters will be more than happy to help you pick a dog that matches your lifestyle.

CHAPTER 3
Preparing to Bring Your Saint Bernard Home

"Sign the puppy up for training class even before your Saint arrives home. Saint Bernards, on average, grow five pounds a week through the first six months of age, so training early is extremely important to instill proper manners before the dog becomes too big."

Jillian Muir
Beech Hill Saints

Before you bring any puppy home, especially one that weighs as much as a small child, you need to make sure that you don't have any clothes, toys, or food lying around where the puppy can get to them. You also need to come to terms with the fact that unless you get extremely lucky, something you like is probably going to get torn up. I can't tell you how many things I found shredded during puppyhood. Sometimes you won't even realize you're missing a shoe until it's gone.

These things are going to happen, but you need to make sure there's nothing harmful within reach. If a toddler can get to it, then the puppy probably can. If you have a puppy in a room with furniture, then keep a close watch on him. It took Tulip a total of one hour to damage one of my end tables past the point of return. Again, these things happen, but you don't want your puppy to ingest cleaning supplies or harmful plastics, for example.

FUN FACT
First Saint Bernard Rescue Dog

Barry der Menschenretter (or Barry the people rescuer, in English) was an early iteration of the Saint Bernard breed and worked as a rescue dog for the Great Saint Bernard Pass Hospice (Holy Order of the Great Saint Bernard Monastery) in the Swiss Alps. It's believed that throughout his life Barry rescued over 40 people. After his death, his body was entrusted to the Natural History Museum of Bern, where he was taxidermized. To commemorate Barry's service, one dog at the Great Saint Bernard Pass Hospice has always been named in his honor. Today, the Barry Foundation, which has taken over ownership of the monastery, is named after Barry der Menschenretter.

Photo Courtesy of
Katrina Anleu

Photo Courtesy of
Victor Gloy

Puppy Proofing Inside Your House

The dangers inside the home can be quite surprising. Items that we pass by every day can be dangerous to a small puppy. You will need to sweep your house a few times to make sure your home is safe to bring a puppy into. Remember that puppies love to chew and want to explore the world with their mouths and paws. This can be a huge hazard if you have cords lying around your house, especially if they're plugged into an outlet. Small knickknacks should also be moved out of the puppy's reach.

If you have any cleaners lying around, then put them in a cabinet or other secure location. Even medication should be put up. Over the counter medication, such as painkillers, can be deadly to a puppy. Scan the room for anything you think your puppy may be able to jump up on and reach. Even curtains or the cord from your blinds can become a target for chewing.

You will also need to identify which rooms are safe for the puppy to go in like the kitchen and what rooms are a no-go like an office with tons of computer wires. A huge aid in keeping a puppy out of restricted areas is a puppy gate. By using a gate, you can moderate what rooms your puppy is allowed in. This allows you to have a smaller area to keep an eye on your new puppy. You can even systematically place pee pads in a contained area to help reduce the damage to your floors.

When you are not able to watch your puppy, you should crate him. This allows you to know your puppy is safe while leaving your home or going into other rooms. With a crate, your puppy has enough room to play and sleep without having access to the rest of your house. When possible, make sure the crate is someplace close to a member of your family, so your Saint Bernard doesn't feel as alone.

Photo Courtesy of Rhonda & Leo Boggs

Puppy Proofing Outdoors

"Check the garden for holes where your puppy could escape. Also, check to make sure plants and garden bushes are not poisonous."

Cheri Moore
Ourfairview St. Bernard's

Along with indoors, you will also want to clean up outside before bringing your puppy home. If you don't already have a dog, then this is an even more important process. Make sure that the area around your house is free of chemicals or chewing hazards. You should make sure that any plants within the puppy's reach won't harm them if consumed. Here are some common plants that are dangerous to dogs:

- Azaleas
- Easter Lily
- Tiger Lily

- Tulips
- Hyacinth
- Daffodils

- Peace Lily
- Daffodils
- Fox Glove
- Morning Glories

Photo Courtesy of
Miaya Foley

If you have a backyard area, make sure there is no trash lying around, like soda cans. Outside toys should also be put up to keep the puppy from chewing on them.

Even the most common outside items can become a toy for Bernards. Tulip especially likes our water hose and thinks of it as a giant flimsy stick. Items that can be chewed through like a water hose are especially dangerous to puppies who could swallow the pieces. Garages should especially be a place of concern as many small items like nails can make their way onto the floor. Chemicals like oil and antifreeze are often common in garages and should be put away. Look for any possible leaks on the floor as they could be from deadly chemicals.

Photo Courtesy of Stephanie Easley

Dangerous Things That Dogs Might Eat

Anything that is not food made for your dog runs the risk of being dangerous if consumed. Even items that are big enough not to fit in your puppy's mouth can have parts chewed off. With Tulip we had a problem with her trying to eat cat toys. In the split second it took the cat to drop a toy it was transporting across the house, Tulip had it in her mouth. Likewise, when we decided to eat pizza with Tulip in the living room, the piece of pizza I dropped was swallowed whole in a matter of seconds.

You should be careful of keeping plastic items, eating utensils, or items with sharp edges around your loose puppy. Likewise, you should avoid eating foods like chocolate near your puppy. There are tons of food like chocolate that are bad for puppies to consume that can easily be dropped on the floor. Some common foods and flavors that are poisonous to dogs are:

- Chocolate
- Coffee
- Avocados
- Alcohol

- Grapes
- Dairy Products
- Macadamia Nuts
- Onions

- Chives
- Garlic
- Coconut
- Citrus

You should even be careful to put up your leashes and stuffed toys. So many dogs end up chewing up their leash or consuming toy stuffing leading to an emergency run to the vet and a costly x-ray.

Photo Courtesy of
Benjamin and Kara Rodrick

Other Household Dangers

Outside of consuming things, there are plenty of things around many households that aren't puppy approved. Here is a short list of common items that can be dangerous to your new puppy:

- Candles
- Wax Warmers
- Portable Heaters
- Knifes

- Guns
- Plastic Cutlery
- Cat Litter
- Paper Towels

For a young puppy, these items can cause clogs in the digestive system that can require costly surgery. Remember that young puppies will be curious and hungry, never assume your puppy is too smart to get burned or consume one of these items.

Setting Expectations for Children

"Teach any children about proper care and handling of the new puppy, and always supervise them. Teach them not to pull on the puppy's tail or ears, and not to poke or squeeze them, and to never, ever hit them."

Dan R Wheeler
Storybrook Saint Bernards

If you have children in your home, then you will need to set realistic expectations for when they meet their new friend. Setting expectations can be especially important with younger children who will get easily excited upon meeting their newest family member. Let your kids know that when the puppy arrives home, it probably won't be ready to play. You will want them to understand that the new puppy needs time to rest and settle in to their new home.

Be sure to teach them not to try and hug the puppy. Many children make the mistake of getting in a dog's face or squeezing the dog. This can upset your puppy and make him scared of your child. You should involve your children in picking out accessories for the puppy, while informing them how to play with, walk, and feed a dog properly. By allowing them to help with the set-up you can let your children feel more involved in the adoption process.

Supplies For a Saint Bernard

Here's where I'm going to take some fun out of the puppy adopting experience. I know you are teeming with excitement over your new pet coming home. You probably have been browsing through all the cute pets products you can find online. Here's a big tip: do not buy anything outside of the necessities. If you do, then you will end up pretty much throwing your money away. These are the supplies you need before getting your Bernard:

- Water Bowl and Food Bowl
- Leash and Collar or Harness
- An Engraved Tag
- Pee Pads, Paper Towels, and Urine Destroyer
- Kennel
- Nail Clippers, Puppy Shampoo, and a Brush
- A Bag of Puppy Food
- A Bag of Puppy Treats
- Teething Toys

Ask your breeder or rescue what brand of food your puppy is currently on to ensure you pick up the right brand. You may also want to ask for neck measurements so that you can get a collar that fits your pet for the ride home.

The Importance of Crates and Kennels

"Get a crate. Crate training is the best way to ensure that the puppy does not get into your belongings and chew them up (which they will for the first year of their life) and will make housebreaking easier."

Jillian Muir
Beech Hill Saints

Getting a crate and possibly even a kennel is essential for your Saint Bernard. The crate will allow you to travel and keep your puppy contained while you not around. Remember that even a three-month old Saint Bernard is going to be decently strong. I suggest going for crates with metal wiring that a Saint Bernard won't be easy to break or chew through. If you want, you can even start with a larger crate and buy a divider to create a bigger amount of space as your puppy grows. A divider is a great way to adjust the kennel without having to spend the extra money it takes to replace them as your dog grows. Most Bernards do prefer to be crated as most crates can be kept close to your family. To give you an idea of a Saint Bernard's needed crate size_ Tulip currently uses a 54 x 36.5 x 44.75-inch crate.

A kennel is a good idea for giving your puppy outside time. If you do choose to install a kennel, make sure it's all metal and can stand up to one hundred plus pounds of weight pushing against it. Saint Bernards are also diggers, so you will need to find a way to make digging out of the kennel difficult. Even if you only plan to leave your dog in the kennel for a short amount of time, place a doghouse for cover and a water bowl inside of it. You never know when a storm could kick up. A large or extra-large sized kennel will be needed to accommodate your growing puppy.

Setting up a Designated Puppy Space

It's best to set up a puppy room instead of having to move the gate from place to place. We used one of our bathrooms to do this. Lay down some blankets and/or a crate, move everything out of the room that isn't for the puppy, and make sure to clean the floor thoroughly. This way, your damage will be confined to just this room, and you can ensure there are no small plastics you have missed.

You will also want to make sure the area is easy to clean. A hardwood or tile floor is preferable in a puppy area, but pee pads can be used. Make sure to not leave your puppy out with pee pads unsupervised as he can tear them up and accidentally swallow them.

CHAPTER 4
Bringing Home Your Saint Bernard

"The first few days after your bring your Saint home, the puppy may seem withdrawn as everything is new to them and they are away from their former litter mates and the people who played with them and fed them. You will need to spend extra time talking and playing with them until they get to know your voice. Speak softly to them and be kind."

Dan R Wheeler
Storybrook Saint Bernards

It's the night before you're going to meet your puppy for the first time; you're brimming with excitement but anxious at the same time. No matter how much preparation you've done, you probably have realized by now that plans don't always go perfectly. I know I didn't sleep the night before we drove to get Tulip. I was up all night just waiting for the morning to come so we could get in the car. I remember we even skipped breakfast in order to get her sooner.

The whole way down, we spent our time throwing names back and forth. We couldn't believe we were finally getting to bring home a Saint Bernard. Little did we know how big of a mess our new baby would make. In retrospect, I wish I would have gotten a little more sleep and had some breakfast on the way. Eating on the way back home while handling a puppy was a challenging experience.

FUN FACT
Rollo Roosevelt

Theodore Roosevelt, the 26th president of the United States, owned myriad pets during his tenure in the White House. Among these pets was a Saint Bernard named Rollo. Rollo was a gift from his namesake, Alfred S. Rollo, who gifted Roosevelt with the dog in 1902 despite Roosevelt's assertion that the family didn't have room for another dog. Rollo loved children and was beloved by them. The Associated Press described Rollo as "a massive Saint Bernard with massive self-restraint."

Photo Courtesy of
Aimee Patton

Meeting Your New Puppy

The night before, make sure to get some sleep, especially if you're driving, and pack some items for the trip. You will want to plan out the route to the breeders home. Make sure you work-in some stops, especially on the way back if you're going to be on a long drive.

Be sure you give the breeder a timeframe for your arrival a few days before your trip. If possible, text them to let them know when you're on the road and when you're getting close to their location. Prior notice will give the breeder time to prepare everything and plan out their day. If you haven't finished paying off the cost of your Saint Bernard, then stop by your bank and withdraw the amount you owe. Cash transactions tend to be much more comfortable when picking up a dog.

Once you arrive at your breeder's kennel, let them know you're outside. Depending on what paperwork you've already filled out, you may need to sign another contract. Many breeders will ask that you sign a contract on pick-up stating that the dog must be returned if for any reason you can't keep it. After the transaction is complete, the breeder will give you a copy of the puppy's records and give you some documents on proper care for the breed. Once all this is settled, you will be handed your new baby.

How to Drive Home Comfortably

Depending on your particular Bernard, you could have a peaceful or eventful trip back home. Tulip mostly slept the whole way back. She was still nervous, however, and had several accidents on the drive home. There are few things worse than being stuck with the puppy runs on the highway. We had to make several surprise pit stops in order to clean up the mess.

I advise anyone who is driving home with a dog to bring wet wipes and plenty of doggy bags. In Tulip's case, her nice wool blanket we brought for the trip lasted a total of 30 minutes. The material wasn't easy to clean off on the go and ended up being disposed of after we got home.

To have a trip with the least amount of hiccups as possible, you should come prepared. You will want to have your crate safely placed in your car. The crate will keep your puppy situated while you drive. Without crating you run the risk of your puppy roaming around your car and being hurt if you have to slam on the breaks. If a wreck occurs the crate will act like a seatbelt and keep your puppy safer from the sudden impact. Before leaving, make sure to line your crate with either pee pads, blankets or a towel. Your puppy will probably have an accident, so make sure the blankets you use aren't your favorites. It's important to protect the interior of your car, trust me, animal stains are no joke. It may be best to opt for old towels that are better suited for absorbing liquid.

Photo Courtesy of
Catherine Koutsoumbaris

You will need to bring some replacement bedding to make sure your puppy stays clean during the trip home. Once you've picked up your puppy, place him in the kennel and give him time to settle down. You will probably want to sit near your puppy if possible to keep a check on him during your trip back. If he starts to stir or whine, then you will want to look for a place to walk him. While you should plan pit stops, it's pretty hard to predict when a young puppy will need a bathroom break.

Photo Courtesy of
Tammy Yarber

Introducing the Puppy Room

Once you get home, you will want to get your puppy settled in for the night. Saint Bernards, in general, are just happy being around people. Their love for family can make your home introduction a little bit easier than with other breeds. Make sure to take your puppy straight to the area where he will be staying for the first few nights. Set him down and stay with him while he explores the room or kennel you've set up.

Don't introduce the puppy to any other animals on the first night. You want him to establish a territory where he feels safe. Once he's checked out his new room, guide your Bernard to his food and water dishes. If he starts to eat or drink, praise your puppy. If you begin praising from night one, training will be more comfortable in the long run.

One thing to keep in mind for the first few nights is that your puppy is going to make a mess. He's also going to make plenty of noise and may get on your nerves. Whatever you do, don't scold your puppy or run to him every time he starts to cry. Your new dog is nervous; it's only natural that he'll chew something up and have accidents. Leaving home is a life-changing moment for your Saint Bernard; his whole routine is completely changing. Be patient as your Bernard goes through this difficult transitional period.

47

Pet Introductions

"Be sure to have your new puppy (or rescue dog) on a leash and introduce them to your current pet in a neutral area (away from the home). When they are both comfortable walk them back together into your home. Be sure to never leave them alone until you are certain they will get along. A new puppy may be too rambunctious for an older dog."

Dan R Wheeler
Storybrook Saint Bernards

The first lesson for your Bernard should be to not chase after the cats. Chasing should be treated as a behavior that isn't tolerated. Bernards aren't the most graceful dogs and can injure a small cat with one pounce of their massive bodies. You will also want to make sure that no mouthing behavior occurs. Even the act of licking can be stressful for cats.

Photo Courtesy of
Lori Brewster

If you already have another dog, then you will want the two to get along. To do this, you will need to introduce the dogs properly and know the signs of aggression. To begin with, only introduce your dogs in a controlled environment. Be ready to break up any possible altercations. Like with cats, it may be a good idea to introduce the dogs to each other's scent first, you may even let them sniff at each other through a gate or door. By introducing smells, your dogs will already be somewhat familiar with each other when they officially meet.

When introducing the dogs, you should be ready to intervene at a moment's notice. Look for friendly behavior like tail wagging, butt sniffing, and playful pouncing. These are all signs that the introduction is going well. On the other hand, if you notice your dog backing up, baring teeth, growling, aggressively barking, or being unusually still, then trouble is brewing. Some introductions between dogs have to be done in sessions before the two can successfully interact in a positive manner.

Introducing older dogs can be a bit harder than introducing a puppy. Use caution and have a towel ready to cover the dog's face if you believe a fight is going to break out. You may also want to use treats to train the dogs to tolerate the presence of one another.

Night Whining

"If your pup is coming from the litter he might cry some at night. Have some good play time before bed, so that he is tired out, and it will help him sleep better."

Van and Beth Pankratz
Pankratz Puppies

Now that you've put your puppy down for the night, you are probably ready to head to bed. The long drive has worn you out along with all the excitement from the day. As you climb into bed and start to close your eyes, you hear the most pitiful sounds. Your Saint Bernard has started whining from being left alone. Now, depending on what your plans are for your Saint Bernard, there are a two different paths you can take.

For us, we knew that Tulip was going to be a mostly inside dog with free roam of the house. So, at 2 am, our hearts broke, and we brought her into bed with us. She immediately crawled down to our feet, curled up, and

Photo Courtesy of
Angelica C. Beaver

started snoring. We realized while watching her sleep that this was probably the first night she had ever been alone. Most puppies will sleep beside their moms or siblings until they are adopted. Tulip was no exception to this rule and didn't understand why she had been left alone in an unfamiliar dark room.

We knew that she'd eventually get big enough to overwhelm our beds, so we gradually increased the period of time she stayed alone each night. Letting her in bed helped to cut down on the whining while providing both us with better sleep. If you don't want your Bernard in bed with you, then it may be best to set up a kennel in your bedroom. That way, your puppy can still see you instead of wondering where everyone has gone.

CHAPTER 5
Socializing Your Saint Bernard Puppy

"Overall St. Bernards are a social a breed. If they are socialized when they are young, they usually are pretty fearless and get along with other pets just fine."

Rebekah Peters
Puppy Pawz

I can't emphasize enough how important it is to socialize any puppy, let alone a Saint Bernard. Your baby is going to grow fast, meaning he'll get harder and harder to teach. Socializing a full-grown Saint Bernard can turn into chaos quickly. While your dog probably isn't going to bite anyone, just his sheer size can cause trouble. Even if you plan to avoid the park or don't want to take your pup on vacation, there are points in time where you won't be able to avoid taking your dog out into the world.

Photo Courtesy of Renate Magnussen

Photo Courtesy of Floyd Gingrich

I can't tell you how many people have been suspicious of Tulip since she's grown up. Even though I know the worst thing she does is drool on my couch, others see a potential danger. Strangers have it in their head that a dog her size could cause serious damage. It's up to Saint Bernard owners to make sure their dogs get the proper socialization they need in order to prevent issues when in public.

When Should Socialization Begin?

After you're sure your puppy is settled in, it's time to begin introducing him to the world. The adjustment period generally takes most dogs a week to two weeks. Even a breed as friendly as Saint Bernards can develop serious behavioral issues when their socialization is neglected. While dogs can be trained at any point in their lives, it's best to start young. Puppies are a lot easier to teach because they don't generally have preconceived notions you have to correct.

For shy puppies, starting the socialization process could be as simple as going for a ride around town or even expanding your walking route by just a few feet each day. For more outgoing pups, a trip to your local pet store can do wonders. Pet lovers are sure to want to pet your puppy, and store employees often give their furry shoppers treats. Positive interaction is extremely important in your puppy's first few interactions and pet stores will offer plenty of this while giving you a chance to talk with other dog owners. Don't worry about your puppy making a mess either. As someone who also worked in a pet store, I can promise you we understand.

Photo Courtesy of
Aga Grzegorek

Introducing Family and Friends

"Start your puppy out young. Get it out at least once every few days in public to be pet by strangers and to experience new and different places. Bring treats with you and ask people that would like to approach your dog to offer it a treat so the dog learns quickly that good things come from being friendly."

Jillian Muir
Beech Hill Saints

If you can set up meet and greet sessions with family and friends in your home, that's great. If you can get permission to take your puppy to their house, that's even better!

By letting people come into your house, you are teaching your puppy that strangers you invite aren't a threat. Having guests over lets your dog know that your home or as he views it, your territory, is open to others. By having the same friends and family meet your dog in your home over and over, you will avoid any aggressive tendencies occurring towards these guests in the future.

It's also essential to take your puppy for visits elsewhere. Visiting other places helps him get used to different settings, making vacations easier in the future. A dog that stays in the same place his whole life can become anxious in new environments. This causes unnecessary stress that can be harmful to both your lifestyle and your dog's health in the long run. A dog that never goes out may have trouble being kenneled or become defensive when introduced to new areas.

Set down some ground rules for any dog-human interactions. When people first met Tulip, they wanted to pick her up, carry her around, and even give her food. All of these were ok with me other than giving her table scraps. While this was cute to my guests, this behavior will teach your dog that it's ok to eat human food. The socialization process should be set up to give your puppy positive reinforcement. Any actions that can cause problems with training or human interaction in the future should be restricted.

Babies and Saint Bernards

Saint Bernards are dubbed the nanny dog for good reason, but should you trust them with your baby? My answer, especially with infants, is a solid no. Tulip is a sweet girl, but she doesn't know her size. She always ends up trying to lean against me or pawing me for attention. For a small baby, this can cause injury. A Saint Bernard should only be around your child under close supervision. Even toddlers need to be monitored or checked on regularly when left alone with any dog.

Children often end up getting in a dog's face or pulling on its fur. While a Saint Bernard may not be aggressive, it might become skittish around your child. If you have a baby, slowly introduce it to your dog like you would anyone else. Over time, your Saint Bernard will begin to understand the boundaries of child interaction. Many Saint Bernards end up being especially protective of children in their families.

Photo Courtesy of
Mary Baker

Photo Courtesy of Ashley Spencer

Cats and Saint Bernards

Cats aren't exactly keen on change in their territory and a huge dog is a big change. It's best to introduce cats when your puppy is small through smell. Take a blanket your puppy uses and put it with your cats to familiarize them with the dog's scent. While there will still be some hissing when the two meet, this makes the chances of a physical altercation less likely. Even our welcoming Sphynx cat Noko had trouble with Tulip. As a puppy, Tulip would grab ahold of Noko by his sweaters in order to play with him. She thought she was just playing, but Noko thought he was about to become a snack. Cats and dogs interact entirely different, and you have to teach your dog this.

The first lesson for your Bernard should be not to chase after the cats. The act of chasing is in a dogs nature. If he does begin to chase a cat break it up immediately and put your dog in time out. Chasing should be treated as a behavior that isn't tolerated. Bernards aren't the most graceful dogs and can injure a small cat with one pounce of their massive bodies. You will also want to make sure that no mouthing behavior occurs. Even the act of licking can be stressful for cats.

*Photo Courtesy of
Debbie Taylor*

Other Small Animals and Saint Bernards

If you have small animals like rabbits, hamsters, or lizards, use caution. While you can find tons of videos of dogs interacting with small animals, it's always a risk. If interaction does occur, it should only be under close supervision. As with cats, a Saint Bernard's sheer size can be enough to cause accidental injury. With small animals, this can be severe, especially when you factor in the common weight of a full-grown Saint.

Let's start by taking a look at common mammals you may have around your Saint Bernard.

> **HELPFUL TIP**
> **The Saint Fancier**
>
> Published by the Saint Bernard Club of America (SBCA), the *Saint Fancier* is the only magazine that is exclusively devoted to this breed. This quarterly publication covers current information about breed research, legislation, special events, health issues, and many other breed-specific issues. Subscription to the *Saint Fancier* is available to members and non-members of the SBCA for a fee. For a publication timeline and fees, visit the SBCA website at saintbernardclub.org.

Hamsters, rabbits, and chinchillas are all common pets. Each one of these mammals is also considered a prey animal. By instinct, your small pets will view your dog as a predator who wants to eat them. Introducing them may serve no purpose and could stress both animals out. If you do want to introduce the animals, do it through your small pets cage. Introducing the animals without the bars in between could take months.

For birds and reptiles, many of the same rules apply. Birds take a long time to build trust with owners much less the family dog. You should keep the two at a distance unless the bird chooses to interact with your dog on its own. If you have reptiles be aware that they are likely to bite at your dog if they feel cornered. Biting is especially prevalent in some lizards and snakes. Keep in mind that many reptiles carry bacteria that could be easily transferable by a friendly lick.

Dog Parks and Outdoor Meetups

Once your puppy has had a few outings and has been vaccinated, then it's time to hit the park. Both dog and human parks are teeming with great socialization opportunities for your Saint Bernard. Make sure to check that the park you want to visit allows dogs.

Photo Courtesy of Lisa Dunn

Before you go, make sure you have a well-fitted collar or harness and a sturdy leash. Chances are your Bernard will be excited to have such a vast new area opened up to him. Expect some pulling on your first park visits and make sure to bring plenty of doggy bags to pick up accidents with.

To start, take your Saint Bernard to a regular park where your dog can walk around and take in plenty of sights and sounds. He will be around a wider variety of people than in a pet store. The goal is to teach your dog not to run up to every human he sees. You will also be able to teach him to deal with distractions, such as other dogs during your visits.

Once your dog is comfortable with a regular park and you decide to visit the dog park for the first time, pick an hour when things won't be too busy. Puppies tend to play rougher than adult dogs, so you will want to keep a close watch for altercations. You may even want to keep your puppy leashed and let the dogs come up to them before giving them free run of the park .

Introducing Dogs at the Park

When you first introduce your dog to other dogs, you should be careful. There are many signs you can watch out for to know if your dog is getting along with the other one. To begin with, these are the signs to look for to ensure you that your Bernard is getting along well with the others:

- Tail Wagging
- Sniffing Each Other's Butts
- Playful Barking
- Running Back and Forth Playfully
- Playful Stances Such as Head Down, Butt Up
- Licking
- Nuzzling

If you notice that the dogs are both raring to play with each other and wagging their tails, then you shouldn't encounter any problems. You may find that your dog needs to sniff another for an extended period of time, or they play pounce for a few minutes before actually tussling with their new friend. This is normal cautious behavior, especially if your puppy has never met another dog outside its siblings before.

Signs the Meeting Isn't Going Well

Just like you can tell that the dogs are getting along well, some signs may point to a possible fight. Some dogs may just not like the company of others or will get anxious from being put around certain types of dogs; here are the signs that the meeting isn't going as planned:

- Ears Back
- Stiff Tails or Bodies
- Tail Tucked Between Legs
- Dog's Staying Low to The Ground
- Growling
- Biting
- Showing Teeth
- Aggressive Barking
- Cowering
- Shaking
- Unwanted Mounting

If you see any of the signs listed above, then you should separate the dogs. Many times, one dog will be excited for the meeting while the other is trying to hide. Never force two dogs into each other's space. If the two dogs don't get along at first, then try to have them meet regularly until they are comfortable around one another.

CHAPTER 6
Living with a Large-Breed Puppy

Most likely, your Saint Bernard won't realize just how big he is for quite some time. This misjudging of his size can become a big problem as your dog ages and rapidly gains weight.

Learning to deal with messes as your puppy grows will help you establish boundaries and teach your puppy good habits. Managing unwanted puppy behavior like inappropriate chewing will play a significant role in their adult life.

Photo Courtesy of Denise Rosa

Photo Courtesy of
Amy Mann

Managing Puppy Damage

My living room wall is proof that a puppy will find something to destroy, no matter how careful you are. Puppies love to explore the world with their mouths. Tulip literally tried to chew on everything; at one point, we found her with her nose squished against the hardwood floor with her mouth fully open. Luckily, she couldn't find a way to chew on a flat surface, but we had plenty of drool to clean up in the spot where she had tried to consume the floor.

The best solution to prevent chewing is to keep a close watch on your puppy and use bitter spray. Pet safe bitter spray will run you $15 a bottle and will do wonders for protecting your furniture. Almost every pet shop carries a variety of sprays that use sour mixes to deter your pet from chewing. If you choose to use the spray, make sure to shake it well and offer your pet a small taste to get them to form a negative connection with the spray's smell and taste. In Tulip's case, she tasted the sour spray once and never attempted to try it again.

Whenever we noticed her licking a piece of furniture, we applied a small amount of spray after telling her no. Keep in mind that if you find the damage well after it has been done, your puppy won't understand why you're scolding him. Simply apply the spray to the area and keep a close watch on your puppy the next time he is close to items he likes to chew on. If you plan to leave your puppy out at night, it's also a smart idea to spray furniture that your pet may chew.

Photo Courtesy of
Linda Beth May

Teething Periods

"Some Saints can be chewers, and with that they may chew the arm rest right off of your kitchen chairs or the siding off of your house. Whenever you cannot watch them they should be in a crate or a kennel, it helps keep them out of trouble and be sure to give them strong sturdy toys."

Marilyn Balikowski
Cornerstone Saint Bernard Kennel

Puppies grow in their adult teeth around the three to four-month age range. Much like a baby, this is a painful time for your puppy and he can become especially restless. The teething period should be over by the six-month mark, but it is a slow process that can drive some pet parents bonkers. To make matters worse, puppy teeth are razor-sharp, which makes it even worse when they start to gnaw on your toes.

Look for these signs to tell you when your Saint is teething:

- Excess Drooling
- Small Amount of Blood on Toys
- Increased Chewing
- Slowed Eating
- Red Gums
- Pawing at the Mouth

During this period, nipping generally gets worse. Your puppy will try to chew on you or anything he can get his mouth around to help relieve the pain. To help alleviate this, you can purchase teething toys specifically designed to help your puppy during this growth stage. It's also a great idea to regularly take a look inside your Bernard's mouth to make sure all teeth are coming in properly. If you reach the six-month point and your puppy is still retaining his puppy teeth, then it's time to see your vet.

During the teething process, make sure your dog is eating properly. If you notice he's in pain when chewing his food, add some water to soften the kibble. You can also feed him wet food. Don't panic if your dog swallows a loose tooth; this is a common occurrence in the puppy world. The tooth will be digested, just like the food in your Bernards's stomach.

*Photo Courtesy of
Buffy Fellows*

Growth Spurts

Growth Spurts are won-drous moments when you wake up in the morning and then re-alize your puppy has doubled in size. While it may not actu-ally happen that quickly, many mornings during Tulip's growth spurts, I would actually wonder if she gained 10 pounds over-night. We found ourselves hav-ing to constantly adjust her col-

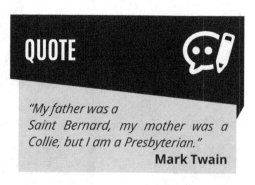

QUOTE

"My father was a Saint Bernard, my mother was a Collie, but I am a Presbyterian."
Mark Twain

lar to fit her neck comfortably, and the amount of space she took up on the couch was constantly growing.

The amount of weight a Saint Bernard will gain each month will vary. Typically a three-month-old Bernard will weigh between 30 to 45 pounds. Each month you can expect your Bernard to gain a minimum of 10 pounds and a maximum of 20. One sure fire way you can tell your Bernard is in the middle of a growth spurt is an increased appetite. Don't be afraid to feed your puppy extra food during this time as he needs it to grow. At first, we were scared to increase Tulip's food, but after a health check with our vet-erinarian, we learned that every dog will have different nutritional needs during puppyhood.

Some Saint Bernards grow so fast that they hit the 100-pound mark at six months of age. A Saint Bernard's crazy growth won't slow until around 12 to 14 months of age. Around the 14 month mark, he will still gain weight, but it will be around the 5 to 10 pound range. By 24 months of age, your Saint Bernard should be done growing, and will eventually reach a weight of 135 to 185 pounds.

Crate Training Tips and Tricks

Kennel Training can be a tough beast to tackle. Some puppies take to kennel training easily while others just don't quite get it. Tulip didn't get it at all; in fact, Tulip was a puppy that would roll around in her own poop. The first few weeks were tough. We'd come home from work to find the happi-est poo covered pup. We'd have to take her out, give her a full bath, brush out her hair, and scrub her kennel. The pooacolypse even happened twice some days, making our daily routine pretty unpleasant. To make matters

Photo Courtesy of
Joann Johnson

worse, even after she stopped playing with her poop, she started eating it to hide the evidence.

Eventually, she stopped thinking it was fun to play in her own dropping and began to avoid it. We made sure to let her out as soon as we came home. This taught her that relief was on the way. You have to keep in mind that most puppies don't have full control of their bowels until around six months of age. There will be accidents in the kennels, and puppy pads aren't always the solution. Trust me, Tulip loved playing with pee pads more than her own toys.

How to Introduce Your Saint Bernard to its Crate

Your dog should see their crate as a personal den. To make them have a positive association with the crate you will need to go through a small process. Making a crate appear as a positive for your dog will begin with picking out their crate at the store. If you pick out a crate that is uncomfortable to the dog, then they aren't going to want to spend much time inside of it. Below is the checklist for picking out the perfect crate for your Bernard; if the answer to one of the questions is no, then look at another option.

Checklist for Picking a Crate:

- Is it made of a sturdy material?
- Is it pet safe with no sharp edges or corners?
- Is the door secure?
- Does the crate come from a reputable company?
- Is it big enough for your Bernard to comfortably turn around in?
- Can your dog stand up fully while in the crate?
- Is the crate easy to clean?

If you pick a crate that isn't well made, then your puppy could get loose or hurt. You will also need to make sure your puppy has enough room to readjust while in the crate. If the space is too small to turn around in, then your Bernard will be miserable. For added safety, avoid any off-brand crates or cheap models that may be made with hazardous materials, such as lead. These crates not only fall apart easily, but they can cause health problems later, especially if your dog chews on the bars.

Creating a Den

Once you have your crate, you will want to create a comfortable den for your puppy. There are a few different ways to make a crate feel like home. If

*Photo Courtesy of
Heath and Melissa Hardy*

your puppy likes to sleep on a bed, then put it into the crate along with a few toys that they are familiar with. By adding items to the crate that already have your puppy's scent, your Bernard will become more comfortable with staying put up for an extended period of time.

If your puppy has a bad habit of chewing up beds or blankets, then use their favorite chew proof toys. As an added strategy, you can leave treats in the crate or give them one each time they successfully go in on their own. Many trainers even recommend that you never reach into your dog's crate while they are in it. By treating the crate like a restricted zone, you are letting your dog know that while they are there, it is their personal space and they won't be bothered.

When you first introduce the crate, don't leave your puppy inside for a full eight hours. Slowly expand the amount of time you leave your puppy in the crate until they are comfortable staying there for hours at a time.

Tips for Using a Crate

One of the best tips I can give anyone is to make sure the kennel isn't too big. A big crate can prompt your puppy to pick a spot to relieve themselves. A small crate doesn't give them an option to create a personal toilet. If an accident does occur, get your dog to come out of their crate and use pet grade cleaners to remove the smell as soon as possible.

You should also avoid using the crate as a form of punishment as your dog can get a negative association with their crate. A negative mindset can eventually make your dog unwilling to be in their crate or even cause them anxiety each time you must put them up for work or sleep.

Finally, if you notice your dog is anxious or can't go to sleep, try placing a breathable blanket over the crate. In many cases, this can help calm your dog and block their view so your movements don't stimulate them when it's time to settle down.

Crate Training No-No's

While a crate is a wonderful way to house your Bernard while you're at work, it doesn't solve all your problems. You should never leave your dog in a crate for more than eight hours, and the crate should never be used as a kenneling service. If you plan to take a long trip, get a pet sitter or board your dog; a crate is not a long-term housing solution.

Additionally, never bang on your dog's crate while they are inside or try to scare them out. By using fear as a removal tactic, your dog will begin to dislike the crate. You should also be careful about leaving food or water in their crate for long periods of time, especially if it's wet food that can go bad. Food can attract annoying pests, like flies, if left unchecked. Additionally, don't use a crate for housing your dog outside, if you plan to house your dog outside, then get a larger kennel.

Managing Bad Habits

"If you do not want your one hundred and fifty pound Saint on the couch, don't let them on the couch while they are puppies. Talking with your family about where the puppy should be allowed to go and what the pup is allowed to do will help, as you will all be working towards the same goal."

Van and Beth Pankratz
Pankratz Puppies

No matter the bad habit, you need to have an action plan to deal with it. Puppy timeouts are a wonderful way to discipline a puppy in a humane way.

Photo Courtesy of Sidney Bennett

If your puppy is nipping or won't take no for an answer, then put him in his kennel for a small amount of time and ignore any whimpering you may hear. This will teach your Bernard that negative actions coincide with unwanted consequences.

Another good tactic is to ignore negative tactics that your puppy uses for attention. If he jumps up, walk away. If he nips or tries to tug on your clothes, ignore him. Never use treats to try to stop behavior like nipping, barking, or jumping. The puppy will associate the treat with the action and will start to act out for rewards. If barking is your main issue, then ignore it when possible. If you live in a sound sensitive area, try putting a blanket over your puppies kennel to calm him down.

Finally, food aggression can be an issue in young puppies that are used to competing with their siblings for food. Even if your puppy doesn't growl or nip when you get near his food, it's a good idea to hand feed him from time to time. Remember that you will need your puppy to get along with others when you go on vacation or business trips. If he feels like his food will be taken away because he isn't accustomed to seeing a human handling it, your dog may become defensive.

Dealing with Drool

Some Saint Bernards will make you a small puddle as they sleep, while others don't drool much at all. Tulip doesn't drool all that much; in fact, she seems to make more of a mess with her water bowl than her mouth most days. Other Saint Bernards I've met are accompanied by an owner carrying a wash rag to clean their pup's face.

Photo Courtesy of Annabella Stephen

Of course, when your Bernard is excited, he will drool more than normal. If you're planning to go out, bring some napkins. Chances are your dog will meet another person or dog that really gets his tail wagging and his mouth salivating. You also never know when, in spite of diligent training, your dog may cover an unlucky stranger in doggy slime.

CHAPTER 7
Potty Training Your Saint Bernard

Potty training can take months to over a year and can test your patience. Repetition, proper training, and a tasty bag of treats will be your best friends during this process.

Patience Is Key

"Patience and consistency is key! Get a crate for the puppy, if you are not watching it constantly ensure the puppy is secure in its crate. When the puppy is young it will need to go out every few hours until it makes the connection between house training and the outdoors."

Jillian Muir
Beech Hill Saints

How long potty training will take truly depends on your puppy; there is no set amount of time for potty training to become completely effective. As mentioned earlier in the book, puppies don't gain full control over their bowels and bladder up until around six months of age. If you have to leave the house for work, then chances are high that an accident will happen during this time period. Even if you take your puppy out every few hours, he may still have an accident.

For Tulip, it has taken over a year for her to finally get potty training down. Our other dog Nate took three months to house train. Don't give up if things aren't working out, just keep your dog on a schedule and notice when he's having accidents, so you can coordinate your schedule to take him out before it happens.

Photo Courtesy of Broderick Balanti and Bryanna Petrick

Never Scold

"After each meal take your puppy outside, praise after each success, ignore any accidents. Never tell the puppy off for a mistake, remember that they are just babies."

Cheri Moore
Ourfairview St. Bernard's

FUN FACT

Saint Bernard Club of America (SBCA)

The Saint Bernard Club of America (SBCA) was founded in 1888. The SBCA is committed to promoting responsible breeding of Saint Bernards and boasts an online pedigree database of over 88,000 dogs. On the SBCA website, you can find information regarding upcoming seminars for education about Saint Bernard dogs as well as up-to-date information about the breed. For more information, go to saintbernardclub.org.

Never scold young puppies for accidents, they honestly can't help it. If you have a puppy between three to five months of age, give them a firm, but calm "no" and take them outside immediately. At this point in their life, they don't understand proper bathroom habits. If your dog is old enough to control their bathroom habits, then you should react a bit firmer. Don't be afraid to interrupt your dog and immediately take them outside.

Remember that your dog isn't designed to work around your schedule. When they need to go to the bathroom it's uncomfortable to hold it. There are tons of things that can upset your dog's stomach, like a new brand of food, or even just a simple upset stomach. A dog should never be yelled at or made to fear you because it has an accident. The old myth of "rubbing a dog's nose in their mess" is also a cruel and outdated way to teach your pet. While your frustration is understandable, you should never direct your frustrations onto your puppy.

If you have adopted an older Saint Bernard, then bathroom incidents may be related to nervousness. In this case, you should treat the newly adopted dog similar to a young puppy. Punishing them may make it harder for them to settle into your home or feel safe. In many cases, adopted pets may have sensitive needs and an unkind voice can make them revert.

Potty Training Reinforcement Techniques

All dogs are a bit different when it comes to training, so feel free to try different methods or mix them together to create a training regime that works best for your lifestyle and pet. Here are some proven techniques for potty training a puppy:

Treat Training

Treat training is the use of rewards to entice your puppy to want to use the bathroom outside. Out of all the training methods, this one is probably

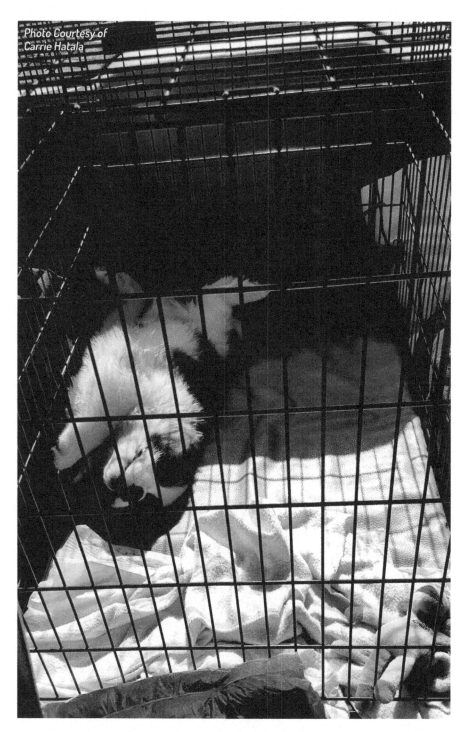

Photo Courtesy of
Carrie Hatala

Photo Courtesy of Joey Uy

the simplest way to entice your dog to use the bathroom correctly. Pick out a treat that your puppy tends to go really crazy for. Then, whenever he uses the bathroom outside, reward him with the treat. Rewarding can be done every single time he relieves himself. Make sure to make these particular treats exclusively for after bathroom usage, so your dog has a clear message of what he needs to do to earn a tasty snack.

JOKE

Bert took his Saint Bernard to the vet. "Doctor," he said sadly, "I'm afraid I'm going to have to ask you to cut off my dog's tail."
The vet stepped back. "Bert, why should I do such a terrible thing?"
"Because my mother-in-law is arriving tomorrow and I don't want anything to make her think she's welcome."

Bell Training

Bell training involves tying a bell on the door. When you take your pet outside or notice your dog giving signs of bathroom-related discomfort, ring the bell and take him out. Eventually, encourage your puppy to ring the bell himself; you may even give them a treat for doing this action. Eventually, your dog will connect going outside with ringing the bell. The bell method works best when combined with the treat method once you get outside with your Saint Bernard.

Pheromone Training

Pheromone training involves putting dog waste in a specific spot outside or using a spray that smells similar to urine. This will let your dog's nose know that this spot is a great place to go potty. For best results, remember to reward your dog with petting or treats when he uses the bathroom in the correct spot.

Schedule Your Outings

I don't think there is a more important factor in potty training then scheduling. Once your dog knows exactly what the potty schedule is, he'll adapt to it accordingly. Make sure to schedule several potty breaks throughout the day, especially when you wake up and right before you go to bed, and after each meal your dog eats. If you only take your dog out a couple of times a day, then you're going to have accidents in the house. The schedule will change depending on your dog's age, of course. Young puppies will need to go out far more often, but the key is still consistency.

Potty Training Aids

For a little extra help during the potty training process, you can choose from a variety of helpful pet products to help cut down on the mess.

Sprays

A good spray will mimic the natural pheromones your dog's urine gives off. By spraying a selected area, you are putting down the scent of another dog. With luck, your dog will feel the need to start peeing in this spot to mark his territory. Keep in mind that rain and snow can wash away the smell of the spray, so it will need to be reapplied occasionally.

Pads

Puppy pads can be especially effective at saving your carpet during the puppy's first few months home. You don't want him to become accustomed to going inside, of course, but they can save you all manner of messes while he's learning bladder and bowel control.

Fake Grass

You're not likely to find a grass patch that will meet the size and waste needs of an adult Saint Bernard, but grass pads can be useful during the early months and can help puppies learn to use the bathroom in the live grass outside. Keep in mind that a fake grass set-up can be expensive and needs to be replaced regularly.

Accidents Happen: Clean Up and Prevention

"Although they grow very fast, their bladders don't. They drink more than they have enough control over...meaning it can take a bit longer to housebreak them than other breeds. They may still even have accidents at 6 or 9 months old. Be patient!"

Marilyn Balikowski
Cornerstone Saint Bernard Kennel

It's generally not enough to just wipe up the mess. If you don't thoroughly clean the area, the dog's nose will prompt him to use it again. Therefore, make sure to scrub, vacuum, or soak whatever has been soiled. Deep cleaning can be a lot of work, but it will cut down on the amount of time you spend cleaning up the future messes.

You also need to keep in mind that Saint Bernards are not to be trifled with when it comes to accidents. These dogs will eventually grow to the point that you are left with cow sized patties of poop. Even worse, they tend to love drinking water and pee a lot. Each time Tulip pees, it's enough to make a small puddle. Saint Bernards grow very fast, and so do their messes, so it's crucial to start potty training the moment you get your puppy.

To better manage the mess and get rid of any lingering pheromones, I highly recommend you invest in pet cleaning sprays. These sprays often have enzymes in them that will eat away at the bacteria that cause the pee smell. There are a variety of these sprays to meet all your home needs. You can purchase cleaning solutions made for fabric, wood, and carpet.

CHAPTER 8
Your First Vet Visits

Getting your puppy to the vet and scheduling his shots is one of the most important steps you can take as a pet owner. As mentioned earlier in the book, you need to find a vet before you get your puppy and possibly even have his first appointment setup.

Not only is it dangerous not to get your puppy vaccinated but many trainers will also refuse to work with you, and getting your dog groomed will be nearly impossible if your dog isn't up to date on his vaccines. Without proper shots, even going to the park is a no-go, as your puppy won't have the needed protection against common diseases that can cause havoc on his growing body. Furthermore, it's likely that you will be contractually obligated in the paperwork you signed with the breeder to ensure you finish the vaccine regimen the breeder will already have started.

Photo courtesy of Lillian & Tommy Williams

Navigating Your First Vet Visit

During your first visit to the veterinarian, you should take the health records that the breeder or rescue provided you. These records will help your vet understand what your puppy is currently up to date on. During your first visit you will also want to schedule his next appointment to make sure your puppy is receiving his vaccines on time.

Additionally, if your pet was on any medicines when you got them from the breeder, then you should bring them with you or write down the details. It also helps to know your upcoming work schedule as you will likely be making future appointments to ensure your dog is getting their shots on time.

Don't worry if your puppy is excited or make a mess in the floor while you are waiting to be called. Puppy behavior is expected by the staff and they will have always tools for clean-up on hand.

What Will Your Vet Check For?

During your first vet check-up, you can expect to have a full examination. The vet will be checking everything to make sure your puppy is in good shape. The procedure will be the same whether you just picked up your Bernard from the breeder, adopted them, or picked them up off the street. Your veterinarian is here to make sure that your puppy is as healthy as the breeder claimed.

Generally, the first thing that happens when you get called back for your appointment is a weight check. The vet will get your Bernard on a scale and make a note of its weight to ensure he's not underweight. The vet will also check the dog's teeth to get an approximate estimate of the puppy's age. By verifying just how old the puppy is your vet can make sure that your Saint Bernard is growing normally. Don't be surprised if your vet checks your Bernard's temperature with a rectal thermometer; this just verifies they don't have a fever.

FUN FACT

Saint Bernards on the Big Screen

The 1992 family cinema classic *Beethoven* chronicles the adventures of a beloved Saint Bernard dog named Beethoven who enjoys a happy life with his human family. But the local veterinarian, Dr. Varnick, has an eye on Beethoven and wants to dog-nap him in order to conduct nefarious experiments. This classic film gained such popularity that an additional seven films have been made about Beethoven the Saint Bernard.

Next, you can expect your puppy to be checked for fleas, parasites, and ear mites. While this may seem like a waste of time, plenty of puppies can pick up pests just by going on a walk outside. Your vet will also take a look at your dog's eyes and gums to make sure there aren't any issues forming. Many vets will also check the paw pads for damage and verify that your puppy's nails don't need trimming.

Finally, depending on your vet, they may check blood work or take a stool sample from your puppy. These are to verify there are no hidden issues in your puppy. You can also expect them to check your dog's legs, torso, and possibly the tail to ensure there are no developmental issues or pain.

Puppy Shots and Vaccinations

Photo Courtesy of Katrina Anleu

Depending on your vet, puppy shots can get a bit expensive. Some vets will have a deal where if you fix your pet, you can get an all-inclusive puppy package that will cost you far less. It's especially important to get your breeder's vet records as your Bernard may have already had a few rounds of shots depending on his age. Here are the standard ages and shots you will need to get:

While Rabies and DHPP vaccines are required, the optional vaccines can be done yearly, as well. I do recommend getting them, especially if your Bernard will be around other dogs. Bordetella is extremely contagious and easy to get from any area where other dogs are present. Lyme can easily be contracted from ticks.

Spaying and Neutering

Unless you plan to breed your dog, it's likely you'll be contractually obligated by the breed to spay or neuter the animal. The last thing shelters need is more unwanted puppies. Furthermore, there are specific reasons why fixing your dog is of crucial importance.

Health Benefits

Healthwise, spaying a female dog helps cut down on the risk of painful UTIs and certain types of cancer. For males, neutering also helps reduce the risk of cancer and prostate problems. In some cases, fixing your pet may even help the dog calm down. Many pets who don't get spayed or neutered also have a higher chance of wandering away from home in search of mates. Wandering is one of the leading causes of dogs getting lost. For females, you won't need to worry about your dog going into heat.

Here are some commonly asked questions about the process:

When Is the Right Time?

In the case of healthy puppies, you may be able to get your Saint Bernard fixed at eight weeks of age. If you have an adult Bernard then schedule a health check with your vet to make sure he is in good enough health to go through the procedure. Senior Bernards may not fare well under anesthesia. Sadly, an older a dog's body is the more likely that anesthesia may react negatively. In some cases, a dog's body will go into hypertension or their heart rate will lower. Most vets will require a senior dog to go through a thorough physical examination do to this procedure.

Cost

Compared to most other surgeries, fixing your pet really isn't that expensive. Thanks to how common the procedure is and the willingness of vets to perform the service, you won't generally spend over $250. Even if you find yourself in a tight spot, ASPCA centers, and other animal welfare organizations offer reduced-price spay and neuter programs that could cost you less than $100.

Spaying/Neutering Procedures

Spaying and neutering is an outpatient surgery. In many cases, you will drop your pet off shortly after the vet opens that morning, and pick him up in the evening. Very rarely do any complications occur that would cause you to board your dog overnight at the vet's office.

Make sure your dog stops eating at least eight hours before the surgery and follow any special instructions given to you by the vet.

After surgery is over, take your Bernard straight home and have a bed set up for him to rest on. Depending on your vet's recommendations and how long it's been since the surgery, you should feed your pet. For the next few weeks, watch to make sure he isn't licking at or pulling on the stitches as this can reopen the wound. Physical activity should be limited and you should administer any pain pills the vet provided you.

Flea and Tick Treatments

I can't emphasize how vital flea and tick protection is. I also can't tell you how many people are confused with all the varieties of medication out there. Not only do you need to worry about picking from a collar, pill, or topical ointment, but you also need to worry about safety. Many flea and tick treatments can become hazardous if the dose is too strong or, conversely, may be completely useless if the dose is too low.

Photo Courtesy of Heath and Melissa Hardy

Make sure that the formula you are picking for your Bernard is appropriate for his age range and weight. It's best to check with your vet during your first visit for puppy appropriate recommendations. Depending on your budget and which medicine type you think works best, there are a few different products to choose from:

Collars: The collars are coated in medicine that slowly releases over a period of time for long term use lasting up to eight months. A carcinogenic chemical is contained in these collars; be aware that this chemical can be damaging to humans and fatal to felines.

Pill: Pills are administered orally to your dog by the vet every three months.

Topical: Topical medicine is the most affordable option and is applied to the back of your dog's neck. Topical ointments need to be reapplied each month. Make sure to separate your animals after using a topical solution to keep accidental ingestion from occurring.

Calming Nervousness at the Vet

Depending on your puppy's temperament, you may find yourself with a nervous dog when you enter the vet's office. For nervous puppies, you may want to schedule an early visit where there aren't as many dogs present. If just the act of being in the waiting room upsets your Bernard, then bring a favorite toy with you. Calming treats are also a good bet, as they use natural herbs to help relax your puppy. Make sure to check the dosage on the bottle before using this method.

If your Bernard is still small, you can also consider holding him or wrapping him in his favorite blanket. Just a kind touch can do wonders for a puppy who is scared of his surroundings. Bringing a favorite toy or treat can be another great incentive for letting your puppy know that he is okay. Make sure to always keep your puppy leashed when he is nervous to ensure he doesn't try to run away or hide.

CHAPTER 9
Loneliness in Saint Bernards

Separation anxiety is a common issue in many dogs. It can begin at puppyhood or develop as your dog ages. Many pets that have been left at a shelter also develop the condition. Symptoms of separation anxiety can range from being slightly noticeable to totally disruptive and dangerous to the dog.

Photo Courtesy of
Victor Gloy

Separation Anxiety

Saint Bernards, thanks to their family-oriented dispositions, are a breed that is prone to separation anxiety. Since Bernards are family dogs, they prefer to spend their time loafing around with you on the living room couch. When you leave, they don't like it, to put it mildly. The risk of separation anxiety increases even more if you have a job with an erratic schedule. Dogs learn to expect to be fed, walked, and other daily activities on a schedule. If you work a job where you're called in at random, or you find that your hours vary every week, then this may upset your Saint Bernard.

FUN FACT
Saint Bernards in Art

When one imagines a Saint Bernard dog, they might think of a dog with a barrel around his neck. This iconic image stems from a painting by Sir Edwin Henry Landseer entitled *Alpine Mastiffs Reanimating a Distressed Traveler*. This painting from 1820 depicts two large dogs and a traveler lying in the snow. There is a barrel around one of the dog's necks that is supposed to contain brandy to revive the traveler. Though this depiction is fictitious and there's no evidence to support that the dogs who traveled the Saint Bernard Pass between Italy and Switzerland carried a barrel of brandy around their necks, this popular image has endured.

Signs and Symptoms

If you are starting to notice unusual behavior in your dog, or he seems excessively uncomfortable when you're leaving, he could have separation anxiety. Here are some possible signs:

- **Destruction of the Home**
- **Holes Dug in the Floor**
- **Excessive Potty Accidents**
- **Constant Whining/Howling**
- **Vomiting**
- **Excessive Chewing**
- **Pulling Out Fur**

Many dogs will use the above-listed behavior to get their owner's attention. Actions such as digging are a good indication that your dog is trying to escape in order to reunite with you. If you're having trouble judging if your dog is acting out more after you leave, then set up a small camera to record his actions.

Photo Courtesy of
Katie Day

What Not to Do When Dealing with Separation Anxiety

If you believe your Saint Bernard has separation anxiety, then you will want to try and ease it. Remember that anxiety is a panic-inducing feeling that your companion has no control over. Behavior such as couch destruction that results from the anxiety shouldn't be treated the same as a regular chewing issue. These attacks are coming from a place of confusion and pain, not from a desire to misbehave.

Never scold your dog for having separation anxiety or try to confine him as punishment. Many people think by adding in a crate or leaving their dog tied outside, they won't have to deal with the destruction. The truth is that by leaving your inside dog outdoors or putting a dog in a crate that's trying to dig his way to freedom is not going to help. You should seek out behavioral training or other alternatives to leaving your dog alone all day. If your dog is causing himself harm, then you need to seek medical help immediately.

Long Work Days and Your Saint Bernard

Most people have to go to work, so how do they handle working with an anxious Saint? To begin with, you should consider how bad the anxiety is. Does your dog just howl himself to sleep, or is he showing signs of potentially dangerous behaviors like digging through a window? If your Bernard has moderate anxiety, then working with him at home is always possible. Simply get him used to the idea of you not being home by gradually leaving for longer and longer increments each day.

If he is still a little anxious when you leave, consider using calming treats. While the calming treat won't work for an eight hour period, it may be just the boost your dog needs to fall asleep after you've left. For more problematic anxiety, you may want to look into dog walkers or daycare. Many dog trainers may be able to help you slowly teach your dog to cope with being alone in a positive manner. You may even be able to soothe your dog just by leaving a blanket you sleep with. Just the scent of the owner can often make a pet feel more at ease.

Remember that the anxiety is based on your Saint Bernard's fear of being abandoned. If you can ease those fears, then the negative behavior your dog is showing will disappear.

When to Seek Professional Help

Sadly, one of the top causes of dogs being surrendered by families is severe separation anxiety. Severe anxiety qualifies as high amounts of destruction to your house and your dog engaging in frantic attempts at escape, possibly even injuring himself in the process. If you've tried supplements, training, and sitters, the problem is likely deeper than a bit of insecurity. Like humans, though, dogs have anxiety medications available that can help them cope with panic.

If you feel like you're at the end of your rope or that you need to be home with your dog 24/7, schedule an appointment with your vet. Many veterinarians are familiar with the signs of separation anxiety and can diagnose your pet accordingly. The vet will also be able to use your dog's weight, age, and health to figure out an anxiety medication that will be effective.

Dog Walkers and Sitters

A dog walker or sitter is a great way to ensure your dog gets more human interaction throughout the day. Many anxious dogs will benefit from having a trusted professional visit them or stay with them during work hours. A dog

Photo Courtesy of
Chelsie Davis

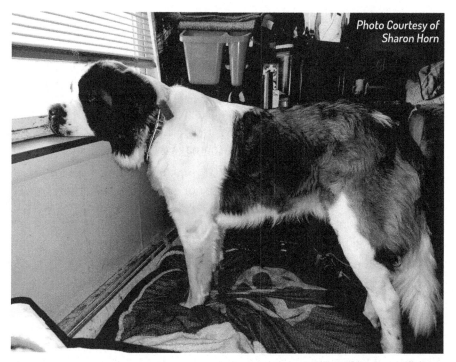

*Photo Courtesy of
Sharon Horn*

sitter can watch after your dog and interact with him throughout the day. Some dog walkers and sitters even offer extra services like cleaning, picking up your mail, or taking your pet for grooming appointments.

Choosing the Right One

Remember that you should be careful when picking a sitter/walker, as you want only the best care for your Saint. Just like with a dog breeder, you need to vet each applicant and verify references. In the case of many walkers and some sitters, these individuals will be entering your home to take care of your pet. Make sure to thoroughly interview each prospective sitter/walker to verify their pet care knowledge and assess their personality. Here are some common questions you should ask:

- **How long have you been professionally caring for dogs?**

- **What is your level of medical training? Do you know dog CPR or wound care?**

- **Do you have any client references I can speak with?**

- **Do you have a business page I can review?**

- **Are you comfortable with large dogs?**

- **Have you ever looked after a large-breed dog before?**
- **What is your emergency plan in case of injury?**

One of the biggest issues I have personally had with boarding Tulip is the lack of overnight sitters with substantial, large breed knowledge. Saint Bernards are big dogs; some people just aren't fully prepared for a large breed. Many Bernards can easily drag a walker along behind them if they decide to chase a bird. Likewise, many sitters may find that watching a large breed in their homes comes with more damage than they initially predicted.

You will also want to make sure that they have a clear plan for action and some basic health knowledge. While not every dog walker may be CPR certified, whoever you hire should at least know how to bandage a wound. Accidents will happen if you take care of dogs regularly, if your walker can't do the basics of pet first aid, would you really trust them to watch your pet?

Finally, make sure to thoroughly check references, business pages, and google their name. If you have a bad feeling or something just seems off, then go with another option. Never leave your home or your Bernard in the care of someone you can't verify or trust.

Doggy Daycare

If you're in a larger area, then you may find doggy daycare centers near you. These centers are often professionally run with a trained staff that knows how to handle your Bernard. Many daycares will offer extended boarding services or even on-site grooming. You may even find that you can schedule classes with a trainer while you're at work. Many busy adults find that doggy daycare can be a much easier process than trying to find a trustworthy individual to watch their dog in their own home.

Keep in mind that doggy daycare is usually a bit more expensive than hiring a sitter/walker. Daycares will also have less flexible hours meaning that night shift workers won't be able to use the service. Be sure to do research on the daycare and check online for reviews to make sure your pet will be in good hands. Many daycares will have hours, services, and basic pricing listed on their websites for you to go over on your own time.

*Photo Courtesy of
Meredith Mansfield*

*Photo Courtesy of
Heath and Melissa Hardy*

Will Getting Another Dog Help?

If you're planning to simply get another dog because your Saint Bernard has developed anxiety, then the answer is no. While having a friend may seem like something that can fix the problem, often, it can lead to more trouble. If you've already been thinking about adding another dog to your home, though, then getting another dog may not be the worst idea. Just don't assume that picking up another pet will magically make your problems go away.

To start with, let's say you get this dog to keep your Bernard company, but it ends up having separation anxiety as well. Now you have two dogs with the same issues, which can cause twice the amount of damage to your home. Some dogs who feel anxious may even end up fighting with one another.

CHAPTER 10
Basic Training for Your Saint Bernard

"Saints can be fairly easy to train. Treats go a long way with them, as does a good rub. Saints like to please so take advantage of that in your training."

Van and Beth Pankratz
Pankratz Puppies

O ne of the most important aspects of owning any breed of dog is proper training. Beyond just teaching your dog cool tricks, your Bernard needs to have basic training for safety's sake. Even if you get your Bernard as a puppy, keep in mind that he will quickly reach the hundred-pound mark. Large dogs can be hard to control if they've never learned basic commands like sit or leave it.

Remember that any dog can be trained no matter how old it might be. Whether you are getting a puppy or rescuing an older Saint Bernard from a shelter, a dog can always be trained. If you ever find yourself in a tough spot, reach out to your vet or trainer to learn about more techniques or to get assistance with helping your pet learn the basics.

Core Training Commands

Core training involves the first steps you should take to teaching your dog correct behavior. Like with all the training we discuss in this book, the most important thing to remember is to be patient. Dogs are creatures of habit and aren't going to pick up a new trick immediately. The amount of time it takes each dog to learn a trick will also vary. Some Saint Bernards will pick up how to sit in a week, but teaching them to stay may take months.

You may find that training a dog is easier with treats or with praise. If your dog responds well to treat training, then pick up a bag of training treats. It helps if these treats are different from the normal treats you use, and you only bring them out as a special reward. By limiting access to the treats, your dog may be able to make a faster connection between his actions and the reward. As your dog starts to get the trick down, you can slowly stop giving him treats.

Photo Courtesy of
Shannon Korte

Sit, Stay, Lie Down, Leave It, Come

These are the most basic commands you can teach a dog. Here are some tips for teaching them to your Bernard:

Sit: Sitting is a great starter trick that will teach your dog to stay still. This is a great trick to learn if your dog often gets excited during feeding time or tries to jump on guests.

To begin, wait until your dog is sitting down, say the word, "sit," and give him a treat. Repeat this process every time you catch your pet sitting down. After a few weeks, your dog will start to associate sitting with both the word and the treat. Slowly begin using the sit command during your daily routine; each time your dog successfully sits, give him a reward.

Photo Courtesy of Linda Beth May

Stay: Teaching your dog to stay can keep him from getting into trouble. Many dogs tend to try and follow you whereever you go. By teaching him to stay, you will have a command that easily communicates a boundary to the dog.

To begin with, go ahead and teach the sit command; this will make teaching stay much easier. Each time your dog sits, repeat the word "stay" until he gets up.

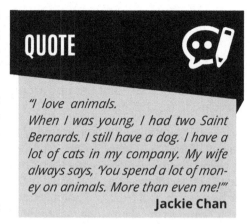

QUOTE

"I love animals.
When I was young, I had two Saint Bernards. I still have a dog. I have a lot of cats in my company. My wife always says, 'You spend a lot of money on animals. More than even me!'"
Jackie Chan

When he gets up, command him to sit once more and begin repeating the word "stay" once more. After a few sessions, begin just saying the word "stay". If you find your dog is still coming toward you, immediately tell him to sit and say the word "stay". This process will need to be repeated for quite some time before your dog begins to associate the word stay with the action of not moving. It can also be helpful to use food when training. Be sure to lower the food slowly while saying the word "stay;" if he tries to take it from your hand or get up, hold the food where he can't reach it, and begin the process over again.

Lie down: Teaching your dog to lie down is a great way to help calm him down. Lie down can be used when your dog needs to be calmed or if he needs to be moved to another spot.

Much like sit, you need to wait for your dog to be lying down. When you see him lying down, give him a treat and say "lie down." As your dog begins to understand this trick, get him to learn the spots he is allowed to lie on with treats. By setting a designated spot for lying down, you can command your dog to move to that spot if they're resting on the couch or in another unwanted area.

Leave It: Leave it is important for getting your dog away from food and any dangerous things he doesn't need to be playing with. Getting a dog to leave it can make walks much smoother if your dog tends to investigate everything around him.

To begin teaching the leave it command, wait for your dog to become distracted by a toy. When he is, say "leave it" and lightly tug the toy away. If he listens, reward him with a treat. Keep repeating this until you notice he is walking away from the toy. You can also use treats to bribe your dog while on walks. Simply pull the treat out and call your dog's name while saying" leave it." Most dogs will be more interested in the reward and will walk away from any trash they are investigating.

Come: Teaching your dog to come to you is a must, especially if he goes outside off-leash. Teaching the come command can be the difference between chasing your Saint Bernard around your yard and quickly getting him back inside for the night.

Depending on your dog, you may find that he will come to you just by saying his name. If he is stubborn or just tend to look at you when his name is called, then you should use the come command. To teach this, say your dog's name followed by the word "come." Use rewards that they can see or hear, such as a treat or squeaky toy. Practice the come command inside your home to get your dog used to being rewarded for his actions. This will let him know that by coming when he is called, he will be rewarded.

By getting down these commands, you can pave the way for a successful adulthood with a well behaved Bernard.

Nip Jumping in the Bud

Jumping is a normal activity that just about every puppy will engage in. For Saint Bernards especially though, jumping quickly becomes a prob-

Photo Courtesy of Maddy Hill

lem. A full-grown Saint Bernard can easily knock an adult down if he gets excited and decides to jump up. Excessive jumping can then make going out in public difficult.

When you bring your puppy home, watch out for jumping. Anytime your Bernard jumps on you for attention, put him on the ground and say "no". You can also opt to turn around or ignore your puppy during this time. You want to teach your Saint Bernard that jumping is a negative that won't earn him attention. The earlier you start to work on this, the fewer problems you will have with jumping as the dog grows.

Shake, Spin, and Fetch

Shake, spin, and fetch are all fun tricks, but should be worked on after the core basics have been taught to your dog. Shake and spin are both tricks that are equally easy to teach. For shake, you simply take your dog's paw in your hand and shake. Afterward, give him a treat, and he will eventually associate the two actions. Spin can be done by showing your dog a treat and then walking in a circular motion around him. With any luck, your dog will follow the treat making the trick a breeze to teach.

Photo Courtesy of
Lillian & Tommy Williams

One of the ways you can encourage learning fetch is by spending time outdoors with your dog. Throw a ball and wait for your dog to grab it in his mouth. Once the ball is secure, call your dog back to you. Getting your dog to come with the ball may take some work, but eventually, he should pick up on the game.

Along with fetch, you can work on "give it." This command can help you teach your dog to release items he has picked up. To help your Bernard learn this, say "give it" when taking the ball out of his mouth.

How to Train an Adult Saint Bernard

You can teach older dogs tricks no matter what the rumors say. Whether you have a Saint Bernard that is three months old or ten years old, training is possible. In fact, older dogs may be easier to train than younger ones as they are calmer. If you're planning on adopting an adult Saint Bernard be sure to ask the shelter about the dog's current level of training. Volunteers should have some knowledge about the dog's grasp on basic commands like sit and stay. You should also inquire about his house-training status to get a full grasp of how much work you will need to put in.

It's important to remember that you should train an adult Saint Bernard the same way you would a puppy. Assume that he has never been shown a trick and start with the basics. By building a solid training foundation, you are giving the adult dog the best chance to learn the tricks without being rushed or harshly judged. Many new owners make the mistake of pushing an adult dog harder when training simply because of their age.

Depending on your adult Bernard's personal preferences, treat training may be just as effective as it is with puppies. If all else fails and the Bernard's size is a little too much for you, then ask the shelter about trainers in your area. Adopting a dog usually comes with access to information about training courses that can help smooth over the rehoming process.

When to Seek Out a Dog Trainer

Seeking a dog trainer is never a bad idea. Whether you just want professional training for your puppy or you've encountered a roadblock, reaching out to a trainer is a great idea. Most professional trainers have gone through dog behavior classes and therefore have more insight into what might be going on in a Bernard's head. This additional insight makes working with each individual dog easier for the trainer than the owner.

Photo Courtesy of Jennifer House

Most trainers will offer several different class types, with obedience training being the most popular. Along with obedience, socialization and out and about classes are also common. Socialization can help familiarize your dog with other dogs and people. Out and about classes can help your dog learn how to behave in public spaces. Keep in mind that most training classes will require multiple weekly sessions.

Many training classes like the ones done at daycares and pet stores are done in groups. If you don't think your dog will do well in a class, then you can also set up private appointments with most

104

Photo Courtesy of
Lauren Moore

trainers. You should keep in mind that most trainers work on a set schedule that may not fit with your lifestyle. Be sure to check with different trainers to find one that can work with your schedule. It might cost a bit more to have private classes, but it can be worth it. In most cities in the US, training classes cost between $25 to $35 per session.

CHAPTER 11
Shopping for a Large Dog

I love Tulip; I loved buying Tulip every cute item I see at the pet store. Sadly though, as my Saint Bernard got older, I quickly learned that you couldn't just buy any old item and expect it to hold up against a large-breed dog. This chapter is intended to help you pick out the best items for your Saint Bernard, without wasting as much money as I did.

Shopping for pets quickly adds up, and stores are designed to have cute items that you want to spend your money on. The problem is that most of these items aren't designed with large dogs in mind. In fact, even some of the items that are supposedly made for large dogs are just for looks and won't hold up for more than a few weeks. Even the basics like buying a good collar can become tricky when you are met with hundreds of options.

Photo Courtesy of Denise Rosa

Buying a Strong Leash and Collar

Whether you have a male or female Saint Bernard, you will find that there are cute collars and leashes in just about every store you go in. For females, you will find tons of designs with bows or jewels on the collar. For males, you will discover camo and baseball prints that look great with your Bernard's coat. Designer collars are substantially more expensive than the plain-looking ones, of course.

Many dog owners will go ahead and pay the extra ten to twenty dollars on the cute collars, at least in part because they think that the extra price means the collars are as durable as they are fashionable. Sadly, ribbons can only withstand so much outside time. No matter how well made they are, the cute bits will often come off after a few weeks of play. As for the printed designs, I've found that many of them will fade after a few months, especially if you regularly clean your dog's collar. To ensure you're buying the proper size collar, you may want to measure your dog or take him with you when selecting it.

Materials like strong nylon and leather can be both comfortable and durable. You should make sure that the buckle is made from a hard plastic that won't snap when pulled on. You can also use chain collars for a short period of time. Chain collars should be light enough for your dog to wear comfortably outside. I recommend close supervision when using a chain collar, as most chain collars are not break away. Chain leashes should also be bought with caution, as you don't want them weighing your Bernard down or possibly causing injury. You should never leave a Bernard tied up on a chain leash, as they will become heavy over time. Likewise, a chain collar can slowly dig into your dog's neck, causing painful cuts.

As for leashes, you will find many of the same problems, but buying a weaker leash is a huge problem when you have a hundred pounds tugging on the other end. I found out quickly that a lot of the "strong" brands just didn't hold up to a large-breed dog. You will really need to look into reviews for leash brands to see how much pulling they can take. Even the more durable looking double braided leashes can snap pretty easily if they aren't made with sturdy materials.

Picking a Harness

Another huge problem with larger dogs is picking a harness that fits. Many of the harnesses labeled large or extra-large simply won't fit. For harnesses, it's best to go into a larger pet store with your Bernard and try the products on. During Tulip's final growth spurt, I found myself taking back quite a few harnesses that I was sure would fit. You should opt for the more expensive brands as they generally fit more comfortably and can last for much longer periods of time. Many hiking targeted brands seem to be an excellent choice for Saint Bernards.

Photo Courtesy of
Linda Beth May

Durable Toys

Another mistake Saint Bernard owners make is buying the quirky toys in pet stores. While Saints aren't bad chewers, for the most part, they still have a mouth full of sharp teeth. Even a gentle tug on a toy's arm by a strong Bernard can cause the stitching to pop. The truth is most toys are made for smaller dogs or dogs who aren't avid chewers, and so even some of the more durable stuffed animals won't be a good fit for a large-breed dog. Even some rubber chews may last only a few days of being played with, especially if they are small.

To keep from running to the toy aisle every week, look for bigger toys. Never buy a toy that looks like it may be swallowed by your Bernard. Avoid rawhide bones, as these can be dangerous when they splinter. Depending on your dog, you should also be cautious of toys with small squeakers or tons of stuffing. Some dogs will just pull out the stuffing, while others will try to ingest it, leading to a possible vet visit.

Thankfully, toy brands have started making lines of super chew toys that come in several different forms. There are stuffed animals made with tough fabric and extremely tight stitching. You can now find rubber super chews that will take months for your Saint Bernard to leave a dent in. Some pet stores even have extra-large, durable tennis balls made for large breeds to play with.

Finding Big Crates

Another frustrating part of searching for Saint Bernard supplies is trying to find outside kennels and crates large enough to accommodate your dog comfortably. Even some of the larger chain pet stores may not carry the sizes you need, forcing you to order your kennel and crates online. This can be an especially frustrating experience as shopping for large pet products online isn't as easy as taking a look at the kennels in stores. A lot of online shopping will be reading reviews to determine the quality of the product.

With crates, you should make sure to only buy them from reputable pet sites or major online retailers. Be sure to check the seller to verify that you aren't getting a product from China, where safety standards aren't necessarily enforced. In recent years many of the popular cheap shopping apps have started to carry pet crates that are unsafe, made of faulty materials, or that come apart easily.

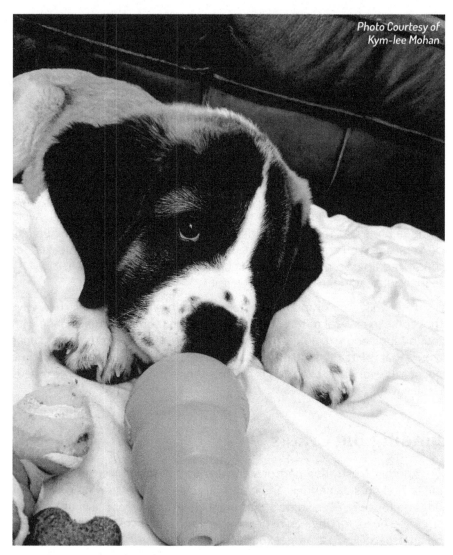

Photo Courtesy of
Kym-lee Mohan

Once you've determined the crate is coming from a reputable seller, check the description to see the materials it is made out of. For a large dog like a Saint Bernard, you will want a sturdy metal enclosure that can't be broken easily. You will also want to ensure that the crate is large enough for your dog to turn around in, and the crate must have ample room for your dog to walk around. To give you a solid idea, the outside crate we are now looking at for Tulip is 6' H x 8' L x 4' W and costs between $250 to $500 depending on the model. We are also opting for covered kennels to combat bad weather.

Extra Large Everything

Not only do you need to worry about giant kennels, toys, and collars, but Bernards will need larger than average food bowls and water bowls. On average, a Saint Bernard eats about six and a half cups of food per day. Most normal dog bowls won't hold even half this amount. I strongly recommend purchasing large food and water bowls made of stainless steel to stand up against your dog's weight.

I also recommend that you always buy the largest bag of dog food, as you will find yourself making fewer trips to the store. On average, Tulip goes through one 30-pound bag of food about every 15 days. Even if you're planning to buy treats or supplements, you may want to check for bags made for large dogs. In fact, even dental treats will have sizes that make them more effective for your individual pet.

Saving Money When Shopping for a Saint Bernard

Buying bigger products means a bigger price tag, making owning a Saint Bernard more costly than a smaller dog. So how do you save money when shopping for a Saint? First things first, I never buy anything unless it's on sale. By waiting for products to go on sale or clipping pet coupons, I cut down greatly on the price of dog toys and accessories. I also regularly check online clearance sections as many toys and accessories often are going out of stock in favor of newer designs. Dogs aren't picky about what toys look like; the cute designs are made to pull in the pet parents.

For example, Tulip's favorite toy is a super chewer eel plush, not because it's a fun sea creature design, but because it looks like a plump stick. Letting go of the aesthetic look of dog products can help you save a ton in the long run. As for supplies like food, it's best to subscribe to your favorite brand's newsletters to get coupons and keep an eye on flyers from pet stores. You should also check to see if you can sign up for a loyalty program that earns you points. Most stores will let you redeem these points for coupons or gift cards.

Finally, check your local pet store's holiday merchandise after the event has passed. You can find many holiday-themed items for cheap since the store is having to move them out quickly.

CHAPTER 12
Common Unwanted Behaviors

"Begging and sneaking are two common bad behaviors. If you don't want your Saint to beg at the table, then don't feed him while you're eating. Being consistent in training will help. If you let him by the table even once while eating, he will always try to be back."

Van and Beth Pankratz
Pankratz Puppies

While your Bernard won't set out to cause you trouble, sometimes unwanted behaviors still form. Luckily, if you catch an unwanted behavior, especially if it's early on, you can work with it. Most bad behaviors can be worked out or significantly reduced with proper training. Be aware that you will probably face one of the common problems listed below at some point while owning a dog.

Obsessive Barking

Saint Bernards are very loud, especially when they get older. Barking with this breed can be especially irritating if it becomes obsessive. This is because most Bernards are so loud that when they are being vocal, you have to speak up in order to have a conversation in your own home. Barking can become even more of a problem if you have close neighbors or live in an apartment complex.

It's important to understand that barking is the way that dogs communicate with us. To begin to work out the problem, you should identify the possible reasons your dog is making so much noise. Does your Bernard not like to be out of your sight? Maybe he isn't getting enough food? If your dog is barking for a completely unknown reason, then take him to the vet. There could be a medical issue.

Once you've identified the reason your pet may be barking, begin working with him. If he doesn't like being alone, leave the TV or a radio on when

Photo Courtesy of
Rhonda & Leo Boggs

Photo Courtesy of
April Souliyadeth

you're not around so that he has some background noise. Placing a blanket over the crate may also help to calm him. You could also consider hiring a dog walker, so he has something to look forward to during the day. If he doesn't seem to be getting enough to eat, check with your vet about appropriate daily food intake.

Food Aggression

Food aggression is one of the nastier unwanted behaviors on this list and is another common reason dogs are surrendered to the shelter. Food aggression can be worked on, but must be done carefully and over a long period of time. Generally, the aggression is stemming from an underlying problem, such as being hungry as a young puppy. Here are some common signs that you may be dealing with food aggression:

- Defensive Stance When Eating
- Growling When You Walk Towards the Food Bowl
- Snapping Over Food
- Eating Extremely Fast
- Standing Over His Food Even When He Isn't Hungry

All of these are signs that your dog may be resource guarding. Understand that negative reactions like scolding or taking away food will likely make things worse. You should never be aggressive to your dog even if he is being aggressive to you.

Remember, never to stick your hands in your dog's food while he is eating. That can be an excellent way to be bitten even by a friendly dog. If you must take your dog's food away, use a long stick to move it out of his grasp. Keep children away from dogs if they show any signs of food aggression.

Breaking Food Aggression

To break your dog of food aggression, you should set new boundaries. Make sure your dog sees you eating before he is allowed to have his dinner. This helps to establish a natural order in your household. Next, play with the dog's food, and pretend to eat it before you give it to him. This lets your dog know that you are willing to share the food and that he doesn't need to be as defensive in order to eat each day.

One of the best things you can do to build trust is to hand feed your dog. Hand feeding doesn't need to be the whole six cups of food your Ber-

Photo Courtesy of
Melyssa Caeti

nard eats each day. Instead, offer a few handfuls of food before giving him his bowl. By allowing him to associate your scent with sharing food, the aggression should slowly start to dial back. You can also try using the leave it command if you need them to drop an item they are being aggressive over.

Food Guarding in Adopted Dogs

If you have adopted a Saint Bernard, then there is a chance he has already developed resource guarding tendencies. In this case, be sure to take everything extremely slow. In some

FUN FACT
Saint Bernards in Horror

In 1981, Stephen King published the now classic psychological horror novel entitled *Cujo*. This book takes place in Maine and follows a good-natured Saint Bernard named Cujo who contracts rabies from a bat bite and goes on a murderous rampage. The main conflict occurs when Cujo traps a mother and child in their car during a heatwave and these characters do everything they can to survive. This classic was adapted into a film in 1983 and won the British Fantasy Award in 1982.

cases, resource guarding is a direct result of abuse or starvation. Talk to your shelter about what behaviors they've been using to safely feed the dog. Some methods above, like playing with the dog's food can feel like a threat to the dog and be potentially dangerous for both of you.

Food guarding doesn't have to be the reason you give up your dog. If your Bernard is food sensitive, then set him up a feeding area and then bring him to the food. Allow him to eat with no disturbances and wait for him to come to you when he's finished. You should also take care not to eat around the dog as food is his main trigger. As for treats, you will want to start by dropping the treat in front of your dog. This will allow your dog to see you as a provider of food without you placing your hand near his mouth. Use patience with your resource guarding dog; with time he should begin to trust you more.

Chasing

Whether it is chasing cars, people, or other animals, this behavior can become frustrating quickly. Chasing is less common in dogs like Saint Bernards that don't have a high prey drive. Unfortunately, these fun-loving dogs may still want to chase your mailman down to give him unlimited kisses. If chasing is a problem during walks, then you may find yourself strain-

Photo Courtesy of
Broderick Balanti and Bryanna Petrick

ing against your dog pulling. Fortunately, chasing can be stopped by learning to shift your dog's attention elsewhere.

If your dog starts to chase, use the core commands to get him to stay. If he successfully stops the chase, reward him with a treat. It will take a few tries to get the chasing to stop altogether, but this method will eventually work fully. In the case of chasing cats, make loud noises to teach your dog that you don't like him chasing the cat. If he continues to pursue your other pets, then take your Bernard to a time out spot.

Yard Destruction

Digging up the yard is something I have had to deal with a lot. Saint Bernards were bred to work and dig in the snow. Digging has certainly carried over in the breed throughout the years, and you're almost certain to find some holes in your yard. One of the biggest reasons for dogs digging in your yard is either boredom or excessive energy. Combating a digging problem can be as easy as spending more time outside with your Saint Bernard or adding in some new outdoor chew toys.

Keep in mind that some dogs, like Tulip, just like to dig for fun. One of the best things you can do for a dirt-loving dog is set up a dig spot. Pick a spot off to the side of your house and dig it up. Fill it back in with loose dirt and use some sprays to attract your dog. Dig spots will allow your dog to practice his favorite pastime without destroying your garden in the process.

Kennel Digging

If you find your dog is digging while in his kennel, then you need a different plan of action. Place rocks around the edges of the kennel or bury chicken wire. If your dog still continues to dig, then seek veterinarian advice as you may be seeing signs of separation anxiety. Immediately remove your dog if he is injuring themselves on these materials and remove the rocks and wire.

Dumpster Diving

When you have a dog, your trash can end up being a prime target for afternoon snacking. There is no magic solution that is going to keep your dog from eating your dinner scraps when you're not home. If your dog starts eating out of the trash, then you need to make it less appetizing or place it somewhere he can't reach it. Remember that wild dogs are scavengers who

*Photo Courtesy of
Adrienne Finney*

use their noses to sniff out a meal, so Saint Bernards, like other dogs, have those same basic survival instincts.

Whenever you have leftovers, you should dispose of them outside of your kitchen trash can. If you do throw them away in your kitchen, be sure to take the trash out later that night. By eliminating the smell of tasty food, your Bernard will be less inclined to dig through the trash. You should also consider installing a dog gate or, if possible, shutting the door to your kitchen when you're not using it. Keep in mind that many types of human food can be dangerous to dogs, especially in large portions.

Common Anxiety

Whether it be barking a bit more when you leave or hiding under the table from thunder, anxiety is common in all breeds of dogs. If you notice that your Bernard starts to shake around loud sounds or when it storms, look into calming items like sprays and chews. Thunder jackets are another popular product used to help dogs who are scared of loud noises. Simply put the jacket on your Bernard if you know it may storm later to help him feel more at ease.

Another huge help for anxious dogs is to make them a special house. This can be made out of a kennel or just in a spare corner of the living room. Put toys and blankets in this area and cover it up. In the wild, dogs live in small dens, and by mimicking this, you are giving your Bernard an extra layer of comfort. Make sure your dog knows the space is his and don't reach your hands inside of the safe space while he is hiding.

Remember that dogs can commonly have bathroom accidents when they get anxious or scared. Never scold your dog for having an accident when he is visibly upset, as this will only make the problem worse.

CHAPTER 13
Going on Vacation with a Saint Bernard

If you own a Saint Bernard and decide to take a vacation, you're going to have to do some planning. Depending on where you're going, you may want to take your Bernard with you. Or, it might be best if he stays at home. This section will focus on making your vacation relaxing for you and comfortable for your Saint Bernard, regardless of whether you take him along or put him in a kennel.

Long Car Rides and When to Rest

If you're planning on taking road trips with your Saint Bernard, keep the following tips in mind:
- Bring Plenty of Water
- Bring Paper Towels for Clean-up

Photo Courtesy of
Tess Colegrove

- Pack Snack Bags
- Pack an Extra Leash
- Plan Out Stops Along Your Route
- Regulate Your Car Temperature
- Don't Leave Your Bernard Unattended

While the first four tips are a bit obvious, the following three are crucial to the health of your pet. Before you even think of setting out on a trip, you should look for dog-friendly parks or rest areas for bathroom breaks. You should try to make a pit stop every 2-3 hours so that your Bernard can get some exercise. Rest stops are also a great chance to provide your dog with a bit of food and water before setting off again.

Photo Courtesy of Jennifer Glenn

Car Safety

As mentioned in the puppy section, it is best to keep your dog in a kennel and restrained while in the car. A Saint Bernard is a larger dog, but you can buy specialty devices to help keep them safe. One of the best options is to buy a harness and seatbelt extension that lets you safely hook your dog into the car without using their collar. This ensures that your dog will be protected during accidents without creating the choking hazard that clipping a collar onto your seatbelt can have.

Make sure that your car doesn't get too hot. Saint Bernards are built for cold climates and can easily overheat. If you notice your Bernard panting, then it's time to cool things off. Likewise, don't leave your dog alone for extended periods of time. If you must get gas or use the bathroom, do it quickly, especially if you're the only one on the trip. Leaving your dog unattended for long periods of time can be dangerous to his health, especially in extremely hot or cold weather.

Getting Used to the Road

If your dog isn't used to riding in cars, then you should take the process in strides. Before going on a car trip, ride out with your dog for a few minutes each day. This can start with short five minute drives around your

Photo Courtesy of Miaya Foley

block and gradually increase by five-minute spans until you hit an hour. You should be aware that some dogs may do better than others in the car. In rare cases, a dog may be motion sick, causing them only to be able to handle short rides without throwing up.

Flying with a Saint Bernard

While not common, sometimes you need to take your Bernard on a plane. In this case, it may be hard to get your Bernard ready for the flight. One of the best things you can do is make sure to get to the airport early to have your dog checked in. You can only fly with two dogs, and your pets must be housed in a strong kennel. If your Bernard seems anxious, then try to give them some calming supplements before you turn them over to the airport's care.

Hotel Stays

"Saints can make good traveling companions, but there are some things to consider when traveling. Hotels sometimes have restrictions on the size of pets and extreme temperatures can make travel difficult too. Remember, Saints do not like hot weather."

Van and Beth Pankratz
Pankratz Puppies

If you are going on vacation, you've probably already started thinking about where you want to stay. It's important to understand that many hotel chains aren't pet-friendly. In fact, you may find it a daunting task to find a pet-friendly location in a smaller area or town. Once you finally find a hotel that does permit pets, don't celebrate immediately. Almost every pet-friendly hotel will have extra policies that limit what kinds of pets are allowed. Sadly, the Saint Bernard is a big dog, and many hotels aren't too keen on the idea of hosting dogs that may weigh more than their staff.

Protecting Your Dog

Before you check-in, make sure that your dog is up to date on all their vaccinations. This can prevent him from getting sick on your trip as he will likely be exposed to more bacteria. You should also ensure that your dog is wearing a collar at all times. The collar should have a tag with your current information just in case your dog decides to run off. I also highly suggest getting your Bernard a microchip before going on vacation. This ensures that even if he loses his collar, a vet can trace him back to you.

Check the Restrictions

Once you find a pet-friendly hotel, read over their description carefully. Here are the two most common restrictions you will run into:

- **Breed:** Many hotels will have a ban on certain breeds of dogs. Large-breed dogs take a lot of room to house, and a hotel may reject your stay if you're not upfront with them about your dog's size.

- **Weight:** Weight is a very common threshold that hotels use to determine if your dog is allowed to stay. Many hotel's max weight limit will be around 50 pounds, and some hotels will only allow dogs under 25 pounds.

The rule of thumb is always to call the hotel to double-check that your Bernard will be welcome.

If you do find a Saint Bernard friendly hotel, then expect to pay a pet fee upon check-in. This can be a small one-time fee of $50, or you could find yourself paying a nightly fee that could run into the hundreds.

Photo Courtesy of Ashley Wilkerson

Leaving Your Dog Alone While Traveling

Depending on the activities you have planned on your vacation, you may be fine with taking your Saint Bernard with you. If you need to leave your pet in your room while you go out, however, then you're going to have to read further into the hotel's policies. Even if your dog can stay in the hotel, there is a high chance that he must be under supervision at all times.

Depending on where you stay, you may be allowed to keep your Saint Bernard in the room alone as long as he is crated. Hotels also generally require owners to hang a door sign stating there is an animal in the room to alert cleaning staff.

Camping with a Saint Bernard

Camping with a Saint Bernard can be a lot of fun; just check with the campsite to make sure dogs are allowed. Once you know you can bring your dog, make sure you have a tent big enough to accommodate both of you. While your Bernard could sleep outside, it's best to have him with you, especially if there are other campers around. If you haven't treated your dog for both fleas and ticks, then make sure to do so before the trip to keep pests away.

If you plan to go into the woods to camp, then use caution. You don't want your Saint Bernard wandering off and becoming lost. Make sure to keep his leash in hand or attached to your waist while you are walking to your site. Once you get there, find a spot for your Saint Bernard to safely wait as you set the tent up. While you're in the woods, we strongly encourage you to let your dog sleep in the tent with you for his safety. You never know what critters may be wandering around your camp while you sleep.

Beach/Lake Safety

Depending on the season, some beaches may prohibit dogs from joining their owners for a swim. If you want to take your Bernard swimming, then we recommend you research beaches that are dog-friendly. You can even find small condos with private beaches that will allow your pets to stay and play. If you're planning to visit during the colder months, then you will find that more beaches allow pets as there won't be any beachgoers to worry about.

If you are planning to let your Saint Bernard swim with you, make sure to be extra cautious. Dogs can swim, but they can quickly get into trouble if

FUN FACT
Porthos and *Peter Pan*

J.M. Barrie, the author of the literary classic *Peter Pan,* owned a Saint Bernard named Porthos from 1894 to 1901. Porthos was a gift from Barrie to his wife Mary, but the dog was very fond of Barrie and accompanied him on his famous Kensington Garden walks where he met Jack and George Llewelyn Davies, the children who inspired the writing of *Peter Pan.* While it was Barrie's subsequent dog, Luath, who supposedly inspired the canine character, Nana, this dog has been portrayed as a Saint Bernard in many of the film adaptations of this book.

the water is rough or they swim out too far. Keep your dog close to the shore, where you can easily get him to dry land in case of an emergency. It's best to pick up a doggy life jacket when going swimming with your Bernard for extra protection. This can be especially crucial if you're taking your dog on a boat ride.

Boat Safety

If you do plan to take your dog on a boat, then be careful. Make sure that he has a life jacket and can swim. While most dogs can naturally swim, this isn't the case for them all. You should also keep from taking your Bernard out if the waters are choppy, as this can be a high-risk situation. If you have a larger boat, you may also want to consider making an area to station your Bernard so that he can be close, but can't access the edge of the boat.

When Not to Take Your Saint Bernard

If you are going to a vacation spot where you won't be able to bring your dog along with you most places, such as Las Vegas, then leave him at home.

If you are going out of the country, you will also have to leave your pet behind. Most countries have a 30-day quarantine period for any foreign animals entering the country. By the time you get done with your vacation, your dog will likely still be in doggy prison.

Should You Board Your Saint Bernard?

If your dog doesn't do well with car rides or being away from home in general, then leaving your Bernard at a dog hotel, resort, or vet's office is a great way to ensure he is well taken care of while you are away. By boarding your dog, you can also avoid having to make your dog spend hours in a kennel while you are away from a hotel room. There are several different types of boarding options to look into, depending on your dog's needs.

Vet Boarding: Boarding your dog at the vet is a great time to get any shots he's behind on and a check-up. While you're gone, the vet office will keep a close watch on the health of your pet. Best of all, vet clinics are equipped for emergencies. Most vets will provide outside time for your dogs, but extra walks can cost more. Your dog is more likely to spend most of its time in the kennel. Many vets are a cheaper option and can board your pet for around $30 to $40 a night.

Pet Hotels: Pet hotels usually allow your dog to stay in a nicer kennel with a few amenities like premium outside time or doggy daycare sessions. This is a great budget-friendly option. Pet Hotels can be a bit more expensive, cost $45 to $85 per night depending on the dog.

Pet Resorts: Pet resorts are luxury pet boarding sites that offer all types of amenities. These resorts may have special pampering packages that include time at the salon or offer in-room pet TV for an additional price. These pricey pads can cost upwards of $80 to $150.

Before you pick a boarding option, be sure to tour the facility and look into reviews from other pet parents.

Boarding Regulations

Remember that there are going to be some regulations for having your dog boarded. Every pet that goes to a boarding facility must have all up to date vaccinations and the paperwork proving it from the vet. You should also check to see if you can bring your own food, almost every boarding facility will recommend you do so to avoid your dog having an upset stomach during their stay.

Using a Pet Sitter

As mentioned in earlier chapters, pet sitters are always an option. If you want your pet to be able to lounge on your couch while you're gone, then you can hire a pet sitter. A pet sitter can come to your home at scheduled hours or even stay in your house while you're gone. If you don't like the idea of a stranger in your home, then you may be able to find a sitter that watches dogs in their home.

CHAPTER 14
Proper Diet & Exercise For a Saint Bernard

"Unless underweight, Saints should never eat puppy food or high protein food, it will make them grow too fast and cause joint and ligament growth issues."

Marilyn Balikowski
Cornerstone Saint Bernard Kennel

Photo Courtesy of
Alisha Chavez

Just like us, Saint Bernards need to have their exercise and nutritional needs met in order to be healthy. Dogs need a balanced diet that meets their individual needs. Saint Bernards, in general, need more food than many other breeds of dogs. For first time owners of a large breed, the amount of food you have to provide to your pet on a daily basis may seem staggering.

Saint Bernard Nutrition

Saint Bernards need a delicate balance of nutrients when they are young to ensure that their bones and muscle mass are growing at the appropriate levels. Adult and senior nutrition is also important to keep your dog's body running properly.

Puppies

Most puppies can be weaned when they are around two months old. At around three months, your Saint Bernard puppy will probably be eating around two cups of food throughout the day. You should gradually increase this amount as he begins to get older. The general rule is to feed a dog no more than it can eat in a ten-minute time-span.

By the time he hits around one year of age your Bernard should be fed six and a half cups of food per day. Some Saint Bernards will eat as little as four cups of food, while others will need eight cups of food in order to not lose weight. You should make sure to split your Saint Bernard's feeding up throughout the day instead of trying to feed him all of his food in a single serving. This can be split up into either two or three feedings depending on what your puppy seems to prefer.

Adults

If your Saint Bernard is below two years of age, you can still feed him puppy food. At this point, your dog is likely still growing, and as you notice his

FUN FACT

The Devil Wears Prada

A Saint Bernard dog made a brief appearance in the 2006 film, *The Devil Wears Prada*, as the pet of the overbearing fashion magazine editor played by Meryl Streep. In the film, Anne Hathaway, who plays the assistant to Meryl Streep, struggles to walk her boss' dog across a New York City street while laden with shopping bags. Dog handlers were on set to hand the dog's leash to Hathaway before crossing the street for the scene and to take hold of the leash as soon as the shot was complete.

Photo Courtesy of
Melissa Castillo

growth gradually beginning to slow down, you should wean him off of puppy food and onto an adult mix. An adult mix cuts down on the calories since your dog is no longer growing. By providing him with a portion of balanced adult food, you can keep him from gaining unnecessary weight.

Senior

Once your dog gets to six years of age, you should consider switching him to a senior formula. This formula is designed to provide your Bernard with the levels of nutrition he needs during his golden years. These formulas won't be as protein-packed and often contain additional additives to help with bone and joint health. The senior formula still has all the vitamins and minerals your dog's body needs to function, but the calorie count is greatly reduced to control weight gain.

Dog Foods: What to Look For

"Saints can bloat, feeding and exercise should never be within the same hour. You can buy slow feeder bowls. Giant breed food with a lower protein is ideal to keep growth slow and steady."

Cheri Moore
Ourfairview St. Bernard's

With any dog food, you should always check the ingredients. Many cheaper food brands will use tons of additives that have no nutritional value to your dog. These foods are the equivalent of feeding your dog an endless supply of junk food. Many nutritionists recommend that you look for foods where the first or second listed ingredient is meat, like chicken or pork. Useless ingredients, such as dyes, should also be avoided as they add no value to your pet's diet.

If your Saint Bernard is below two years of age, you can still feed him puppy food. At this point, your dog is likely still growing, and as you notice, his growth gradually beginning to slow down, you should wean him off of puppy food and onto an adult mix. Puppy food is generally higher in protein than adult foods, as puppies need extra nutrients to grow properly.

Once your dog gets to six or seven years of age, you should consider switching him to a senior formula. This formula is designed to provide your Bernard with the levels of nutrition he needs during his golden years. These

Photo Courtesy of
Renate Magnussen

formulas won't be as protein-packed, and often contain additional additives to help with bone and joint health.

There are many different types of food you can feed your Saint Bernard. Whether you go with dry food, wet food, or a raw diet is up to you. Keep in mind that the fresh diet and a raw diet can be more pricey than traditional dry and wet foods.

Dry and Wet Food

You shouldn't feed your Saint Bernard just one type of food. A healthy mix of both dry and wet canned food is recommended by many nutritionists. By feeding both soft and hard foods, you can help maintain your dog's dental and digestive health. Both foods also have their pros and cons when it comes to storage and cost. Dry food is usually cheaper to buy and much easier to keep stored. On the other hand, wet food also has higher nutrition values since it has to go through less processing than kibble.

Ideally, you should try and feed your dog a 50/50 mix. This will give him additional daily hydration from the canned food, while hard food helps to keep teeth clean.

Fresh Food

Fresh food diets have become more popular, and now you can buy refrigerated pet foods in many grocery stores around the world. These foods are prepared fresh and then sent out in sealed packages to be stocked in the freezer aisles. Fresh food typically has a short shelf life and can be more expensive to feed your dog then dry and wet food brands. On average, feeding Tulip on a fresh food diet can easily cost us $150 a week.

Raw Diet

In addition to the standard diet, there are raw recipes. Many people have found that the raw diet tends to be better on their dog's stomach. The raw diet usually uses raw meat, including organs, to make a dish for your dog. This may turn some owners off, but the raw state of the products can help enhance your dog's coat. Raw diet costs can vary, as many who practice the diet will own a farm or hunt to gather the ingredients. Owners must also be selective about the ingredients they use as raw meat can contain bacteria and parasites.

Specialty Foods

If you have a Bernard with special dietary needs, then you will need to look into special foods. Luckily, there are many brands that offer a large variety of formulas for you to choose from. If your vet doesn't think you can find what you need in the pet store, then they can write you a prescription for specialty food that will be tailor-made to your Bernard's health problems. Here are some common types of specialty foods that can be found in pet stores everywhere:

Photo Courtesy of
Angela Royalty-Hicks

Dental Health: Dental formulas are designed with special ingredients that help keep your dog's teeth clean. These formulas are great for pets who experience dental related issues such as cavities or gingivitis.

High Protein: If you have a pet that seems to be on the skinny side, then look into high-protein foods. These formulas can help a skinny Bernard gain weight fast.

Skin and Coat: These formulas are made with ingredients that naturally add shine to your pet's coat and skin. They can be great for pets suffering from dry skin or yeast infections in some cases.

Weight Loss: If your Bernard seems to be packing on the pounds, then switching to a weight-loss food will help. Weight-loss formulas are designed with reduced calories to help your pets feel full while still losing weight.

Weight Control

Weight gain can be a problem for dogs who take in more calories than they burn. Senior dogs can put on weight more easily since they have a decreased amount of activity. If you notice that your dog is starting to gain a significant amount of weight, then it's probably time to change his food. You can either choose to go with a diet food for a short amount of time or try to convert to a senior formula. Both of these options can help your dog slim down, but you should consult with your vet before making any major changes to your Bernard's diet.

If you notice that your Saint Bernard is still gaining weight after switching his food, then he could have a thyroid problem or drastically decreased metabolism. In these cases, your vet will have to run some tests to come to a proper conclusion about your dog's weight gain. Never cut your dog's food portion suddenly; if you must reduce the food amount, do it gradually over the course of a few weeks.

Common Food Allergies

Many Saint Bernards can suffer from common food allergens such as grain, corn, or even gluten. While these are rare allergies, they aren't completely unheard of. If you notice your dog vomiting, developing rashes, or having liquid bowel movements, then a food allergy is a likely culprit. Here are a few helpful food types for dogs with allergies:

Gluten-Free: Believe it or not, it is possible for dogs to be allergic to gluten. There are plenty of gluten-free dog food brands out there to choose from in your pet's favorite flavors.

Grain-Free: While pet nutritionists are still debating whether grains are good for your dog or not, there are still some dogs allergic to wheat. If your dog seems always to get an upset stomach, then try switching to grain-free foods.

Sensitive Stomach: If your dog always seems to end up sick no matter what food you try, then pick up a formula for sensitive stomachs. These dog foods contain easy to digest ingredients perfect for Bernards of all ages.

No matter what food you think you may need, talk to your vet before switching your dog's diet. A veterinarian can check your dog for possible allergies and help direct you to the best pet food brand for your Saint Bernard.

Treats to Avoid

Just because you can buy a treat, doesn't mean it's good for your Saint Bernard. In fact, you would be surprised how many dog treats are made with unhealthy ingredients. Even some innocent-looking treats can be a choking hazard that should only be offered to your pet when he is supervised. Make sure to thoroughly read the packaging treats come in to make sure that they won't upset your dog's stomach; dog treats can be made with everything from healthy pumpkin to useless food dyes.

Many treats will use the name natural or healthy in the title, but the ingredient list will be full of by-products like corn and chicken meal. Don't fall for advertising campaigns that simply try to make money off of health-conscious dog owners.

Don't Buy Rawhide

The most common and risky treat you can feed any dog is rawhide. For years cheap treats have been made from rawhide and sold in pet stores all over the world. Not only is rawhide not healthy, but it can be a major choking hazard for your dog. Saint Bernards, along with other large breeds, are at increased risks as they may accidentally swallow rawhide treats whole, leading them to choke. Even under proper supervision, rawhide has been known to break off while being chewed on injuring the dog.

The treat is also often made from leftovers in the slaughterhouse and can have very little quality control. Because of this, it isn't unlikely for rawhide to make your dog sick. The AKC recommends washing off the treat before giving it to your dog. It's also important to keep in mind that rawhide is treated using a plethora of chemicals.

Worst of all, you won't know how well your dog can digest rawhide until they've already eaten it. Rawhide is a food that a Bernard's stomach can't easily break down, and in some cases, your pet could be left with a painful tummy ache due to the slow digestion process.

Exercise

"Don't overdo exercise where it puts undue stress on their joints until they have stopped growing at around two years of age. A lot of hip problems can develop through improper exercise during this time."

Rebekah Peters
Puppy Pawz

Every good diet needs exercise thrown in to help balance things out. Saint Bernards aren't high activity dogs, but that doesn't mean a short daily walk is enough to keep them healthy. Saint Bernard puppies should start out with a limited amount of exercise of around 15 minutes a day. As your puppy gets older, you should gradually increase this time span until he is getting an hour's worth of exercise each day.

Saint Bernards, in particular, are a breed that can easily run into bone and joint issues later in life. You should heavily limit the amount of exercise your dog does, especially early on, to keep any excess damage from occurring to their bodies. Saint Bernards should never exceed an hour of activity; most dogs can get away with around 45 minutes of exercise and stay healthy. Long periods of running can wear on the dog's muscles and joints. It's also a good idea to give your Bernard bone and joint supplements to help him stay healthy.

In addition, you will probably notice that your Saint Bernard gets quickly tired out even when they are young. Many Bernards will play games like fetch for around ten minutes before sitting down and panting. This is normal as their large bodies can easily get hot, and they haven't been bred to exercise for hours on end.

CHAPTER 15
Caring for Your Saint Bernard's Hygiene

"Get ahead of grooming from day one. Get your puppy used to scissors on feet fur, and use a dog blaster regularly. A quick brush regularly is much better than trying to brush a tangled dog."

Cheri Moore
Ourfairview St. Bernard's

A‌ll dogs need to be cared for appropriately when it comes to their grooming needs. When a dog isn't groomed properly, it can end up with painful mats and uncomfortably long nails. Most dogs, especially breeds like Saint Bernards, can't naturally take care of their own coats. You also need to make sure that your dog gets regular dental care. Likewise, you need to care for your Bernard's ears as wax and dirt can build-up, causing discomfort.

Photo Courtesy of Robin Herzberger

Photo Courtesy of
Tonya Hudson

Summer Grooming

Depending on your dog's coat type and the area you live in, you may also need to consider getting your Bernard's hair clipped. Having a groomer shave down your dog's coat during the summer can help keep him cool, especially if he likes to spend most of his time outdoors. If you're planning to get your dog's coat shaved down, then plan to do it at the beginning of the summer. This will ensure your pet stays cool throughout the warmer months.

When it gets close to the end of August, you should avoid getting your dog shaved, as he needs to grow back his natural coat for the winter months. Keep in mind that most groomers won't shave young puppies. Also, bear in mind that no matter how short your dog's coat is, he can succumb to heatstroke.

Photo Courtesy of
Denise Walkingstick

Dealing with Matted Hair

Mats are going to eventually happen whether you brush your Bernard's fur every day or not. Most mats will be small as long as you make sure to care for your Saint Bernard's coat properly. Smaller mats can often be worked out of the dog's coat with little to no pain. If you don't brush your dog's coat regularly and mats are left for an extended amount of time, then they will become harder to remove. In fact, mats can get so bad that they have to be carefully shaved out of your pet's coat by an experienced groomer. If the mats are bad enough, you could find yourself paying a high grooming bill for the extra care it will take to shave down your Bernard's fur safely.

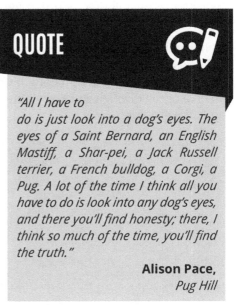

QUOTE

"All I have to do is just look into a dog's eyes. The eyes of a Saint Bernard, an English Mastiff, a Shar-pei, a Jack Russell terrier, a French bulldog, a Corgi, a Pug. A lot of the time I think all you have to do is look into any dog's eyes, and there you'll find honesty; there, I think so much of the time, you'll find the truth."

Alison Pace,
Pug Hill

Causes

Mats are generally a combination of shed and unshed fur. Mats often happen more during the hot months of the year when your dog is starting to shed his winter coat. If you have a Bernard, then you've probably noticed that he has an undercoat. This means that as he sheds, hidden mats can form in his coat that you might not catch in your next brushing session, no matter how diligent you may be.

While shedding season is prime time for mats, they can also form if your Bernard likes to play in the rain or snow. Just like human hair, a Saint Bernard's is more likely to tangle when it's wet. Because of this, you should try and thoroughly dry your dog off when he's been playing in the rain. This may also be a good time to brush him after he's dried to ensure no mats are forming in his coat.

Working Out Mats

Don't fret if you discover a mat in your dog's coat. There are plenty of ways to easily remove them when they are small. For starters, you should purchase a dematting brush. These fine-toothed combs are designed to pierce through the mats to help loosen up the hairs. They are easy to use, and within a few minutes, you should be able to work the mat out of your dog's coat safely.

In combination with the comb, you can also pick up a dematting shampoo. These shampoos work just like a conditioner to soften the hair help break up mats. Using a dematting brush and shampoo at the same time can help break through stubborn matted fur to help save you from a costly trip to the groomers.

Photo Courtesy of
Linda Beth May

Bath Time

One of the most common mistakes dog owners make is bathing their pets too much. In truth, you should try to bathe your Saint Bernard no more than once a month. Bathing him any more regularly will cause his coat to lose important oils. Without these oils, you will notice that his coat will look less healthy and his skin can become irritated and flaky. That being said, if your Bernard has an accident or comes home covered head to toe in mud, then giving him a bath is a must.

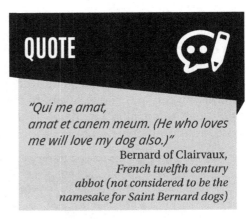

QUOTE

*"Qui me amat,
amat et canem meum. (He who loves
me will love my dog also.)"*
Bernard of Clairvaux,
*French twelfth century
abbot (not considered to be the
namesake for Saint Bernard dogs)*

Bathing Tips

Bathing a full-grown Saint Bernard can quickly turn into a disaster if you're not careful. From Bernards that become afraid of baths to ones that have to make a splash into your tub, bathing can be tricky. Here are some tips for successful Bernard bathing:

Start Young: Begin bathing your dog every month after you bring him home. While he is small, you can train him to like baths and practice proper etiquette when in the tub.

Supplies to Have Ready: Make sure to have your shampoo, rinsing cups, and towels in place before you bring in your Saint Bernard. If you have to go through your house searching for a towel, then chances are high you will come back to a soaked bathroom.

Make Baths Fun: You can buy a toy or special treats to make bath time fun. This can be a great way to get your dog to turn or sit still while you're trying to scrub his belly or paws.

Consider a Pet Washer: Pet washers don't require you to run a bath, making washing your pet easier. Most washers can easily be installed to your shower and have settings to adjust the water flow.

Test the Water: Before putting your dog in the bath, you need to make sure the water won't burn him. Your pet's bath should feel lukewarm to the touch. If you think the water feels a bit warm, then let it cool down a bit before bathing your dog.

How to Bathe Your Saint Bernard

To bathe your Saint Bernard, you should follow the tips above to set up a proper bathing area. This will allow you to get your Saint Bernard in the tub quickly. You will want to wet your dog's fur thoroughly and then apply shampoo. Each Bernard is different in this regard and your shampoo usage may vary. Try to start with a palm-sized amount of shampoo and add more later if you run out. You will want to start by scrubbing the shampoo into your dog's torso; after you have his upper half thoroughly soaped, move onto his tail and then his belly.

Photo Courtesy of
Amanda Willis

Next, gently pick up each leg so that you can wash the paw pads. This is also a great chance to check his nails to see if they need trimming. Once the dog is lathered, wash him off and begin by starting on his head and face. By saving this area for last, you are more likely to avoid getting soap into his eyes. You can also use your free hand to shield his eyes as you scrub around them and rinse out the soap. Be sure to be ready for immediate shaking and grab a towel to dry off your pet.

Cleaning Your Bernard's Ears

Along with making sure your dog's coat is cared for, you also need to worry about the ears, teeth, and feet. Saint Bernards are floppy-eared dogs that can easily get dirt and debris trapped in their ears. When not cleaned, this can cause discomfort and even infection. Pests like ear mites can also start to accumulate in a dog's ear if they spend time exploring through weeds or bushes outside.

Check your dog's ears weekly to see if they need cleaning. Gently use a cotton ball and pet safe ear cleaning solution to wipe any dirt away. Never use a Q-tip or try to push the cotton ball too deeply into your dog's ear canal.

Teeth Cleaning

Next, you will need to tend to your dog's teeth regularly. Just like humans, dogs can get cavities and build up excessive plaque. You can find dental supplies at many pet stores and should start brushing your pet's teeth as soon as you bring him home. You don't need to worry about sifting through many products as there are only a few brands of toothpaste, and they are all vet recommended. In addition, you will need to choose a toothbrush that has big enough bristles to clean your Bernard's teeth. Many dog toothbrushes come in standard form and finger form so that you can attach the brush directly to your hand. To ensure your Saint Bernard is getting the proper amount of dental care, brush his teeth two to three times every week.

To begin brushing his teeth, slowly lift his gums and lightly scrub his teeth. You should work your way down his mouth by rubbing in circular motions. You may need to do this a few times before your dog sits still for a full brushing.

Nail Clipping

Photo Courtesy of Beverly Oliver

You will need to pay special attention to your dog's feet, mainly his claws. Dogs claws are always growing, and if they don't get worn down, they can become painful. You should have your dog's nails clipped at least once a month to ensure that they aren't growing to painful lengths. If you have chosen to clip your pet's nails yourself, be sure to educate yourself on where your dog's nail quick is located so that you don't injure him. Make sure you get a large pair of dog clippers from your pet store. Having a container of styptic powder is also essential when clipping nails to stop any bleeding that could occur.

Once you have everything set-up, grab your dog's paw and lift it gently. You will need to lightly squeeze each toe to get the nails to pop out. Carefully look over the exposed nail for the quick, this will be a dark blood vessel that can be seen easily in clear nails. Make sure to leave a small amount of room in between the clippers and the quick. Once you are absolutely sure you're not going to damage the quick, cut the nail and repeat the process until you finish each paw.

Professional Groomers

Unless you're a groomer yourself, I highly suggest enlisting the help of a trained professional at least a few times a year. Groomers are especially useful when you need to shave your pet's coat down or need to trim his nails and can't tell where the quick ends. If your Bernard has a hard time fitting in the tub, or you simply can't handle the bathing process, then a groomer can help. Most groomers have access to large tubs and special tools to help keep your pet safely held in place while being washed.

Groomers can also give your pet a deeper cleaning and have the tools to give them a more precise cut. If you notice that your dog often gets worked

Photo Courtesy of
Ashley M. Tuzikow

up when being groomed, then there are plenty of vets that can use anesthesia when grooming is absolutely necessary.

Choosing a Groomer

Just like with choosing a vet and a pet sitter, you should take special care when looking for a groomer. Check the reviews of the shop and ask for references if the groomer runs their own business. If you need an in-home groomer, then use one of the many sites that let professionals safely communicate with clients. These sites will always have a review section where you can closely examine feedback from other pet owners.

CHAPTER 16
Basic Saint Bernard Health Care

Owning a dog means you're going to have to visit a vet regularly to ensure that they are healthy. Saint Bernards can't talk to alert us to injuries or clogged ears, but your vet can check for these issues during appointments. We've already gone over the first few vet visits, but what happens when your Bernard gets older? How often do you need to visit the vet? This section will tell you all you need to know about basic health care for your Saint Bernard.

Remember before giving your pet any new health products to always check with your vet.

Annual Check-Ups

Making sure your Saint Bernard gets his annual check-up is extremely important. Annual check-ups let your veterinarian gauge your pet's overall health and check for any underlying issues. Many vets will be able to identify and test for breed-specific issues that commonly affect Saint Bernards. Make sure you always schedule your annual visits a few months ahead of time to guarantee you can get your dog in on time each year.

What exactly happens at an annual visit? When your dog reaches adulthood, he should have an annual visit to update his shots and do an overall examination. To begin with, the vet will weigh your dog to make sure he isn't over or underweight. Then your Bernard will often be checked for ear and dental health.

Depending on your vet, they may take blood or stool samples to check for common diseases and will likely take a look at your pet's eyes. An annual visit is also a great time to talk about aging Bernard's health issues; your vet will likely inquire about his movement in order to gauge if your Bernard is developing any bone or joint issues. Before you leave, you should look into getting the proper dosage of heartworm pills for the year, along with flea and tick preventives.

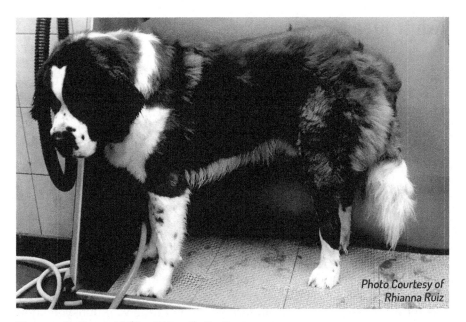

Photo Courtesy of
Rhianna Ruiz

Breed Specific Health Issues

"Saints have some problems; Hips and elbows especially. Many breeders will claim they have no problems but the truth is that 46-48% of Saints eventually have hip problems according the OFA foundation. Look up the Saint Bernard Club of America's web site (https://saintbernard-club.org/), they have a lot of information on health concerns."

Dan R Wheeler
Storybrook Saint Bernards

While Saint Bernards have many common ailments that can affect them in their senior years, like seizures, the breed has very specific issues that most Bernards will end up facing later in life. The biggest issue is skeletal dysplasia, especially elbow or hip dysplasia. This issue causes Bernards' bones to become disjointed, making walking, running, and especially jumping painful.

Heart problems are also common in the breed due to their size. Saint Bernards often have problems with heart flow later on, which can cause them to suffer from heart attacks. Finally, they can have tons of gas. While this may seem cute, excessive gas is painful to the dog and can cause them to avoid eating.

Adult Flea and Tick Care

Unlike heartworm medicine, flea and tick care can usually be purchased over the counter in most places. As mentioned earlier in the book, there are many companies offering different types of flea and tick care for your pet. You will need to choose between one of the many products and make sure to keep your dog up to speed with his dosages. Having proper flea and tick care becomes even more crucial as an adult as your Saint Bernard will likely spend even more time out of the house than he did when he was a puppy.

Types of Worms

One of the most common health issues seen in domestic pets, like cats and dogs, are worms. These parasites can come from a variety of places, including a bug your dog just so happens to swallow while running. While your vet can treat for heartworm year round, there is currently no preventive for other types of worms. In fact, you will have to wait until you know your pet has worms to really do anything about it. With that being said, here are the four common types of worms dogs can get:

Hookworms: Hookworms can be contracted by licking the ground or digging in the yard.

Photo Courtesy of
Renate Magnussen

Tapeworms: Tapeworms are extremely common and often break into segments; these worms can commonly be ingested when your dog consumes a flea.

Roundworms: Roundworms are more typical in puppies and can cause slowed growth.

Whipworms: Whipworms can live in stale water or contaminated dirt; dogs get this parasite by ingesting a contaminated object.

Each of these worms can ultimately lead to death or organ damage that can make the dog have a poorer quality of life.

FUN FACT
Health Research

A portion of the funds raised by the SBCA Charitable Foundation supports research into correcting health issues faced by Saint Bernards. In 2019, this foundation sponsored a study conducted by the Morris Animal Foundation which investigated a new immunotherapy approach to preventing metastatic osteosarcoma in dogs. Osteosarcoma disproportionately affects large-breed dogs such as Saint Bernards and is one of the most painful and deadly diseases faced by this breed. For more information about this study and the SBCA Charitable Foundation's other causes, visit their website at sbcacharitablefoundation.org.

Even in less severe cases, worms can lead dogs to become severely underweight and malnourished. Left unchecked, each of these parasites will continue to multiply until they take over the host's body and kill them.

Worm Symptoms and Care

Worms are easy to identify and have some very clear symptoms that appear seemingly out of nowhere in pets. If you see any of these signs, then you should seek out a vet to test your pet for worms:

- Lethargy
- Loss of Appetite
- Bloating
- Diarrhea
- Vomiting
- Itching
- Scooting
- Weight Loss
- Poor Coat

If you have identified that your dog has worms, then head to your vet or local pet store to pick up some medicine. Many worm medicines simply need to be administered once to take care of the parasites. Make sure to check with your vet if this is your first time dealing with worms in your Saint Bernard. If you have a puppy younger than the recommended age on the bottle, then check with your vet for safe treatment of the worms.

Natural Care Alternatives

If you're more holistic-minded, then you may want to look into natural pet alternatives. While many of these alternatives can't take the place of steroids or antibiotics, they can help with minor issues like anxiety, stress, or even muscle pain. Alternative care options for your pets can include supplements, aromatherapy, acupuncture, music, and even professional doggy massages. Depending on the resources available to you, these alternatives can be cheap or run you upwards of a $100 per session.

Acupuncture: Acupuncture is the process of using needles to activate pressure points in your dog's body. If you have a Bernard who is suffering from chronic muscle pain, this method may help alleviate the pain. This is a procedure that can be risky if not done by a licensed professional since needles are being used on your dog's skin. Make sure to check the facility's license and look for reviews online.

Photo Courtesy of
Kallie Brock

Canine Massage: Dog massage has become more popular over the years. A massage parlor for dogs can often be found at many grooming salons and sessions take around 30 minutes. While in the massage, the therapist will work on kneading the muscles of your dog and work out any knots that may have formed. It's important to note that while most dogs enjoy massages, a more hyper Bernard may not work well with their masseuse.

Aromatherapy: Aromatherapy is done by using lavender and chamomile oils to help relax your pet. To do this, simply purchase an oil diffuser and a pack of lavender or chamomile oil. Follow the instruction on the diffuser to add the proper amount of product. Within 30 minutes to an hour, the oil should start taking effect.

Music Therapy: While music's effects vary, many pet owners leave on soft tunes to help calm their pet's anxiety. This can be done by using tracks with soft instruments like flutes.

Health Supplements

Starting vitamins and health supplements early on can help pave the way for a healthy life for your Saint Bernard. Many over the counter supplements can be bought that help with everything from proper stools to shinier coats. As with human supplements, you must make sure to provide them on a daily basis and it can take a few weeks to months before you start to see any real results.

You also should remember to check supplements to see if they have any restrictions. Some supplements and vitamins can only be taken for a few months at a time. If you're looking to give your Saint Bernard an extra boost in health, then check out these common supplements.

Bone and Joint

The most popular supplements for Saint Bernards are ones that help with joint and hip care. Large dogs, in general, are more prone to hip dysplasia and common issues like arthritis. These supplements are often loaded with calcium and glucosamine. By adding in a supplement, you can strengthen bones over time to make your Bernard's risk of bone-related issues decrease. Keep in mind that proper exercise amounts are still crucial in helping your Bernard to stay healthy.

Skin & Coat

Skin and Coat supplements are great for dogs that have dry skin or often get rashes. These supplements are generally packed full of vitamins like vitamin D, vitamin C, and Vitamin E. Each of these vitamins works to provide the skin and hair follicles with the extra nutrients they need to stay healthy,

Urinary & Kidney

Urinary supplements may not be that important when your Bernard is young, but can help out later on in his life. Urinary supplements help keep the urinary tract clean and deter UTI's from forming. Many of these supplements will contain familiar ingredients like cranberries and marshmallow root.

Before using any supplement, you should consult with your vet, especially if your Saint Bernard is already taking medicine. Each dog will have different reactions to different types of medication. If you notice any excess scratching or your pet begins to vomit, then you should seek out veterinary care and avoid giving him any additional dosages of a supplement.

Common Health Complications

As with any dog, Saint Bernards can suffer from some common but easily treatable health complications that you can look out for. Here is a list of the most common health issues and how to treat them when they occur.

Heat Stroke

Heatstroke occurs when your pet is left in a hot area for too long and becomes incredibly dehydrated. Common symptoms for this condition can be frothing at the mouth, lethargic behavior, dry nose, excessive panting, and in some cases, shaking. To prevent this, make sure your Saint Bernard has plenty of shade and water on hot days. Never ever leave your dog unattended in a hot car or room.

Kennel Cough

Kennel cough is extremely common if you allow your dog around other dogs or have just brought him home from the shelter. If your dog gets kennel cough, isolate him from other dogs and give him time to rest. If his coughing or breathing becomes worse, seek out a vet immediately. Some common signs of kennel cough are coughing, sneezing, nasal discharge, lethargic behavior, and a small fever.

Photo Courtesy of
Ali Miller

Respiratory Infection

Respiratory infections are similar to a bad cold and can have your dog wheezing, coughing, and sneezing all over the place. If you notice these symptoms, take your pet to the vet as he could need antibiotics or a steroid shot.

Yeast Infection

Yeast infections occur when natural yeast starts to grow uncontrollably on your dog's skin. You can often tell if your dog has a yeast infection by excess scratching and a strange smell akin to corn chips. Yeast infections can be caused by allergies, and you should immediately consult your vet to find the cause of the issue.

Constipation

Constipation is a common issue in many dogs. If you have noticed your dog seems uncomfortable and hasn't pooped, then he may be constipated. Talk to your vet immediately. It may be easily resolvable or could be indicative of something far more serious. There are many over the counter medicines for stool softening, and, after getting the all-clear from the vet, you can give your dog a tablespoon of pumpkin to help get things moving again.

CHAPTER 17
Senior Saint Bernard Care

As your dog ages, new issues will arise, and you will need to offer him a more tender type of care to keep him thriving. You should understand that an older Saint Bernard often needs special care to get through the day comfortably. Generally, Saint Bernards are considered seniors at around six years of age. You may notice that your pet isn't as active, or he just prefers to sleep the day away. Both of these are natural parts of becoming a senior that you will learn how to deal with below.

You should also consider visiting your vet for check-ups more frequently to ensure your pet is staying in good health. A vet can do a senior exam to make sure your dog isn't suffering from any issues like hearing loss.

Photo Courtesy of
Semmler Horky

Orthopedic Beds

Even with the best supplements and exercise restrictions, your Bernard will likely have some trouble with his bones as he ages. Sleeping on a hard floor will only amplify these problems, and even your couch may not be equipped to help give your pet a comfortable napping spot. If you want to provide your senior dog with a great place to sleep, then you should look into buying an orthopedic pet bed.

Orthopedic beds use quality materials like memory foam to create comfort layers that make the beds easy to rest on. While you may have to special order a large enough pet bed for your Bernard, they are well worth the price. Be wary of any orthopedic beds with cheap price tags, as these often won't last long or won't have the comforting effects you are looking for.

FUN FACT
The Barry Foundation

The Barry Foundation was founded in 2005 and shortly thereafter took ownership of the Great Saint Bernard Pass Hospice breeding kennel. The breeding kennel is 300 years old, and as such is the oldest Saint Bernard kennel in the world. The Barry Foundation aims to preserve the Saint Bernard breed as well as the traditional hospice dog. They believe that "Saint Bernards from the hospice are both a Swiss cultural asset and a symbol of the friendship between man and dog." For more information about the foundation and its endeavors, visit the website at fondation-barry.ch/EN.

Even if you end up not getting an orthopedic bed, make sure your Saint Bernard has a soft surface to sleep on. Even a regular quality dog bed or a blanket is better than sleeping on a wood floor.

Keeping Motivated

Another huge problem many owners run into with older Saints is a reduced desire to exercise. Even in old age, getting off the couch is extremely important to keeping your dog healthy. If your dog isn't running to the door for outside time like he used to, then you might just have to encourage him. Many owners will make the mistake of assuming they should let their senior dogs spend more time indoors. While he may need to rest more, your senior Saint Bernard should still be getting around forty-five minutes' worth of exercise.

If your dog tends to just sit after a few minutes of walking, then try to use a toy or treats to get him up and moving. You may want to take your dog to a park he likes so he will be encouraged to walk more. You may even find that by simply running with your pet, he will be more than happy to join in. Saint Bernards are family dogs and, even in old age, will want in on all the fun activities.

Be sure not to push your senior dog too hard. If your Saint Bernard is panting early on or just lies down and won't budge, then it's probably time to head home. Like all senior animals, your Saint Bernard will have days when he just might not be up for a long walk. If your pet seems to be in pain from moving around for extended periods of time, then check with your vet. The dog is likely experiencing joint or bone pain and anti-inflammatory medications can be prescribed to help them get moving again.

Mental Exercises

You should also take care to make sure your Saint Bernard is still playing with toys. Even if he doesn't have the energy to play fetch like he used to, you can buy brain teasers. These toys will keep your Bernard's mind active while providing him with hours of play. Some teasers include food puzzles and treat puzzles that force your dog to work for his prize.

Bladder Control

Photo Courtesy of Kate Sittenly

As your dog gets older, his bladder control will likely get worse. You should be prepared for common issues like incontinence that can cause your dog to have to pee suddenly. While this can be treated with medicine or surgery, some dogs just can't hold their pee for as long as they used to. If you notice your dog trying to get you to take him out more, then don't just assume he wants to play. Many dogs will gradually start to need more frequent bathroom breaks as they enter their senior year.

If you find that you just can't accommodate the bladder issues, then you can look into doggy dia-

pers. While this can be a bit messy, many owners use diapers to help their dogs stay inside when they become seniors. Diapers can be used while you're at work or around the clock to make sure no accidents occur. Keep in mind that using diapers does mean you will need to clean your dog by wiping away messes or giving him a full-blown bath. If he soils himself greatly, this may need to be done daily.

It's important that you don't scold your senior Bernard for accidents he can't control, as this will just stress him out further. You should also keep from putting your Saint Bernard outside full time to avoid messes. A dog that has lived his whole life inside may not fare well when he's suddenly made an outside pet. Senior dogs also have a harder time dealing with cold and hot weather.

Hearing and Vision

The older a Saint Bernard gets, the less he may be able to see or hear. If you notice your dog bumping into more obstacles, then his eyes may be affected. If your dog seems to be losing his vision, then you will want to walk him on a leash and take him to familiar areas. Inside the house, you should avoid moving around furniture or food bowls as he may have a difficult time adjusting. If you must move something, make sure to take the time to show your dog its new location.

Hearing loss is another common issue that older dogs may face. Don't get frustrated if your pet doesn't come when you call. Just like with vision, you will need to find ways to work around your dog's hearing troubles. This

Photo Courtesy of
Amanda Daniel

can be by using a strongly scented treat to get his attention or even using a special sound to get him to recognize when you're calling for him.

No matter what issue your dog has, you should take care not to scare him. Dogs with hearing or vision loss may not be able to sense your presence as easily. Be sure to find a way to let your dog know when you come home or when you're passing by. This can be as simple as giving him a treat or a gentle pat on the head. Keep in mind that growling is natural if an older dog is startled.

Ramps and Doggy Stairs

As mentioned in the previous chapters, Saint Bernards tend to have joint and hip problems as they age. These painful issues can make simple tasks like getting on the couch painful for your dog. If your dog takes longer to climb on and off the couch, or he has stopped trying to lie anywhere but the floor, then he may need some assistance getting up and down. In this case, investing in doggy ramps and stairs is a great idea that can help your Bernard keep resting in his favorite spots.

Doggy stairs and ramps can be bought in a variety of heights to accommodate any type of dog. For Bernards, slanted ramps may be easier to climb than trying to navigate up a set of stairs. Before buying any items, make sure to check the weight limit as many products aren't made for large breeds. You should also try to buy ramps that can be easily moved, as these items can help your Bernard get in and out of cars for vet visits.

While these items can usually range into the hundreds, most people can't safely carry or pick-up a Saint Bernard. Many movable ramps and stairs are made so that they can easily be stored so that they aren't in the way when not in use. As a bonus, these products are often made out of durable materials that will last for years to come.

When It's Time to Say Goodbye

An unfortunate part of having any pet is saying goodbye. It is an inevitable part of life that we must come to terms with before it happens. For most people, they are more than a pet; they are part of your family. The death of your pet can have a huge emotional impact. People have different ways of coping with death, but make sure you take time to grieve properly. Make sure if you decide to get another pet, you don't rush into it just because you are grieving. Give yourself at least a month's time to adjust.

Deciding on Euthanasia

Euthanasia is an extremely difficult decision to make and should not be taken lightly. It is an option for dogs that are terminally ill or critically injured and are in so much constant pain that it is more humane to let them go peacefully. If you decide on it, you should talk to your vet about exactly how it is carried out. There are options to have your pet euthanized at home in a familiar setting for them, but a trained veterinarian or euthanasia technician has to perform it in most states. Always consult your local laws and be completely sure it's the best decision before you decide to euthanize your pet.

Remembering Your Friend

There are many ways of memorializing your Saint Bernard after they pass so that you and your family will never forget your loving friend. Once your pet has passed, a veterinarian will talk to you about options you'll have for your pet. One of the more popular options is cremation. This allows you to keep the ashes of your pet in an urn or memorial box. Another option is to bury your beloved pet at home in a memorial plot. Our Saint Bernards will always be with us in memory, but this gives you a place to "visit" your furry friend.

Made in the USA
Coppell, TX
22 September 2022

83515238R00090